This book is to be returned
... ...
... ...ing Scotland

Storytelling Scotland

A Nation in Narrative

Donald Smith

Polygon

Polygon
An imprint of Edinburgh University Press Ltd
22 George Square, Edinburgh

Typeset in Baskerville by
Hewer Text Ltd, Edinburgh, and
printed and bound in Great Britain by
Mackays of Chatham, Kent

A CIP Record for this book is
available from the British Library

ISBN 0 7486 6310 X

The Publisher acknowledges subsidy from

THE SCOTTISH ARTS COUNCIL

towards the publication of this volume.

for Alison

Contents

Acknowledgements

Behind this book lie many years of listening to storytellers, ranging from people in communities all over Scotland who know and care for their history and environment to the great Scottish Traveller tradition bearers. Some of their names will be found in these pages, but I stand in debt to all of them and have not forgotten a single one.

But I would also like to thank my teachers at Stirling High School, Professor Alec Cheyne of New College in Edinburgh, Hamish Henderson of the School of Scottish Studies, Naomi Mitchison the author, Professor John MacQueen my PhD supervisor, and Donald Campbell the playwright and critic, all of whom have shown me something of how richly interconnected our cultural environment is and why, for a Scot, Scotland is the right place to begin our exploration. Many other researchers and creative writers have opened up the fertile territory of Scotland in recent decades and they are acknowledged in the course of my narrative.

Acknowledgements are due to The School of Scottish Studies of the University of Edinburgh for permission to quote from archive transcriptions of ballads and stories by Jeannie Robertson, Stanley Robertson, Willie McPhee and Betsy Whyte; to Duncan Williamson and Linda Williamson for permission to quote from *A Thorn in the King's Foot*; to the estate of Sorley Maclean for permission to quote from 'Hallaig'; and to Collins Publishers for permission to quote from *A Search for Scotland* by R. F. Mackenzie. I also acknowledge, in Chapter 5 'Making Sense?', a debt to the pioneering work of Dr William Donaldson and Professor John MacQueen.

Finally, I would like to thank all my hardworking

colleagues at The Netherbow, past and present, including the artists, actors, poets, playwrights, puppeteers and story-tellers who are the creative frontline of Scotland's cultural endeavours. Marjory Carnegie deserves a special thank you for patiently word-processing successive revisions of this text, as do Alison Bowden and her colleagues at Polygon for their careful editing and production.

I feel a great sense of relief in getting this book on to paper since it says something about the importance of storytelling which has needed to be said, for some time. However, for the way it is said and to what effect I must take sole responsibility.

Donald Smith
January 2001

Introduction

◆

Narrative is a way of ordering our experience and understanding: *a* follows *b* follows *c*, though somehow *d* may have to be fitted in as well. The story involves active agents who will and desire and do, as well as the world of nature and impersonal forces or circumstances which may limit or produce action. The narrative does not convey random discrete units of experience but a pattern that connects people, events and place. There is a sequence of linked happenings through time.

In this sense, storytelling and story making are core human activities without which we cannot function. Certainly narrative is fundamental to mythology, religion, culture and, in the post-Darwinian era, to science. Everything, it would appear, is a process through time and to make sense of it we have to make stories. The extent to which we as perceiving humans impose such narratives on the world around us, as well as our experience, and the extent to which we elicit the narratives from something 'out there' or 'in here', remains problematic. But, whatever the status they are accorded as fact, fiction, scientific theory or divine revelation, frameworks of narrative interpretation are vital.

Stories are sequences in time but they are not time-bound. This is because they encapsulate memory and memory is the human faculty which works constantly to instil emotion, meaning and value into the sequence of happenings. Memory both makes connections through time and strives to turn time's process to a human purpose. In this way, memory is basic to all human culture but it is seen in a very pure and concentrated form in oral storytelling. If I tell you a story without a written script or external cues, then it is entirely dependent on what I can remember at that moment and on whether the act of communication or sharing between us as human beings is effective. The results are always interesting since what is memorable to the teller and what is communicable to the listener are intimately related. They tell us a lot about each other and about our cultural and community contexts.

Such interaction over a period of time constitutes an oral culture or tradition, binding the personal and the social into a unified pattern. Traditional oral cultures have exercised a fascination long after modern technology appears to have rendered them obsolete. In reality, purely oral transmission is very rare; most cultures have been influenced in some way by recorded materials. Even before the advent of writing, visual and synaesthetic records, such as cave paintings, rituals and even star patterns, played a part in storytelling. However, whatever the mix of media, where oral storytelling remains, memory is seen at work in a very distinctive form. Such oral traditions consistently produce exemplars of the storyteller's art.

It is also now clear that, where human memory can be exercised and shared, oral storytelling can be recovered and revived even in a technologically driven society.[1] This happens both because people react consciously against the depersonalisation of technological dependence and because technology itself has subverted written records and created its own instant oral culture in the broadcast media. In both cases, the quality of memory is intrinsic to the quality of communication.

Perhaps, in an age of information overload, oral storytelling remains as important as ever before in human culture. Personal acts of memory and oral communication reaffirm the primacy of human capacities and values, and offer vital clues to attitude, identity and culture on individual and collective levels. Storytelling stimulates memory through both the visual and verbal imagination, making people both better communicators and better listeners or interpreters. This constant transaction between the creative storyteller or story maker and the imaginations of those who receive the stories builds community and may underpin a capacity for shared vision and action. The personal feeds the collective while the storytelling collective nourishes the personal. Many other art forms can draw on such narrative experience.

Oral storytelling, therefore, can be an instrument of personal development and a former of social values in traditional and technological cultures. Storytelling exercises memory, stimulates mental development,[2] brings people into contact with each other and counteracts the corrosion of trust and identity inherent in an economic system driven by impersonal mechanisms and objectives. Storytelling gives us back our ability to see ourselves and each other as characters in connected narratives.[3]

The discussion of Scottish storytelling in this book is cast in the light of these general issues. Scotland is rich in oral traditions which, in purely oral and recorded forms, have been vital to the survival of distinctive Scottish identities. In the twentieth century, a revival of interest in storytelling was one part of a cultural renaissance and of the reassertion of political identity which led to the creation of a Scottish Parliament in 1999. Moreover, within that renaissance, oral storytelling cross-fertilised with literature, theatre and film-making. But, as a small northern European country, Scotland remains uncomfortably stretched between the impersonal imperatives of the global marketplace and the attractions of local identity and sustainability. We remain a culture in transition to we know not where, which is what renders our story making compulsively interesting to ourselves and, hopefully, of some significance to a wider humanity.

Notes

1. *The Scottish Storytelling Forum Report for 1999–2000* indicates that over 150,000 people participated in an organised storytelling session in Scotland. *Storytelling in Scotland: The National Directory of the Scottish Storytelling Centre*, (2000) Edinburgh: The Scottish Storytelling Centre, profiles seventy storytellers working full- or part-time in Scotland in the year 2000–1.

2. For a convenient non-specialist summary of the latest research on the operation of the brain, see Robertson, Ian (1999), *Mind Sculpture*, London: Bantam.

3. See Sennett, Richard (1999), *The Corrosion of Character: The Personal Consequences of Work in the New Capitalism*, London: Faber & Faber, passim for a sociological analysis of the erosion of coherent identity due to the loss of connected narratives.

Folklore, Myth and Legend

◆

Two motivations or interests tend to drive oral storytelling. On the one hand there is the need for a cultural geography – a desire to place the interaction between environment and history in known locations, and to express the importance of nature within the framework of cultural memory. Land and environment shape the story while stories influence how we see the world of nature. Oral traditions reflect a collective mentality, world view or vision in which nature and environment play a dynamic rather than a passive role.

This background is pervasive and powerful, but the foreground is more precisely verbal and decisive in catching the listeners' immediate attention. Incidents, metaphors, crises and descriptions help both tellers and listeners to explore the variety of human experience, to experiment with identity, to find their own voice and story, and so to establish their place in the world. But these personal stories are held within a wider narrative frame, relating our experience to the kaleidoscope of humanity. Individuality is part of a universal patchwork.

In serving these twin goals – environmental association and human significance – Scottish storytellers have formed narratives and narrative traditions with little regard to academic distinctions between myths, legends, folklore and history. These genre categories imply some form of judgement regarding the truth status or function of different kinds of stories. But the makers and receivers of oral narrative, past and present, are much less concerned with applying external criteria than with the truth-to-experience of any narrative, its practical capacity to further personal and group values, and its potential to entertain. The coherence and dynamic of the narrative itself will determine its acceptability among communities of listeners. Without such inherent narrative viability expressed in character, structure and images, a story cannot emerge and be sustained. Unless it is told and retold, and formed by such telling, the story will fade from memory.

Scottish folklore often transmits an older dimension of mythic belief and ritual. Sometimes this survives in a fragmentary form because the continuity of tradition – oral and written – has been obscured, but in other cases there is a remarkable completeness. Bennachie, for example, in Aberdeenshire is a location whose natural distinctiveness and historic importance have perpetuated older traditions.[1]

The name Bennachie is Gaelic and means 'the Hill of the Breast' which accords with the Scots name for its principal summit, the Mither Tap. The female principle or the personification of a mother goddess is retained across Scotland in place names and associations of the *cailleach* (Gaelic) or carlin (Scots). Such connections are sometimes balanced by a maiden well (often dedicated to St Bride) or some other representation of female youth. It is no surprise that an outcrop on the Mither Tap is called the Nether Maiden or alternatively the Maiden Craig.

Bennachie is also the location of the Maiden Stone, a Pictish carved monument whose rock type matches the Mither Tap. This stone, which may have marked a ritual boundary in the approach to the prehistoric site of Bennachie, is now the marker for a remarkable story in which a young woman is wooed by the Devil. Despite being promised to another, she jokingly agrees to accept her dark suitor if he can construct a stone causeway to the Mither Tap before she runs through her supply of meal for baking the bridal cakes. As the realisation dawns that this impossible task will be accomplished, but not by mortal agency, the maiden flees towards Pittodrie Wood pursued by the Devil and, crying on the point of capture for heavenly help, she is turned to stone. And there she bides to this day, a monument in stone, just as the remains of a prehistoric causeway still lead towards the fortress of Bennachie.

The link between the mother, the maiden and dealings with the Devil in the Bennachie lore is interesting, given the historic identification or misidentification of fertility cults with black witchcraft. At Airthrey near Stirling, for example, the Witches Craig (where women suspected of witchcraft were reputedly put to the test by being thrown from the cliff) is known on older maps as the Carlie Craig.[2]

Masculine forces too are at work in the shaping of landscape and Bennachie is also home turf to a famous giant, Jock o Bennachie. Features of the mountain are identified with the giant's bed (Little Johnnie's Length) and even with his drying green (Johnnie's Sark). In addition to these domestic pursuits, Jock o Bennachie maintained a longstanding feud with his rival, Jock o Noth, who occupied another notably isolated peak, Tap o Noth, thirteen miles to the northwest at Rhynie. There various massive rocks are the result of the giants' ballistic prowess, complete with gargantuan finger and toe marks.

However, on one occasion, the two gigantic Jocks combined forces to loup to London and rescue 'Lang Johnnie Moir', a youthful giant who had been unjustly imprisoned in the English capital. Despite this successful joint expedition the undoing of both giants was the still powerful feminine principle or at least the big men's inability to cope with women. Jock o Noth dies in one story in the embrace of his rival's true love, squashed under an unprecedented Bennachie missile. The other Jock, however, also succumbs to female enchantment and is still imprisoned in a cave under the mountain, awaiting his freedom. Local prophecy maintains that:

> A mither's ae son wi ae ee
> Sall fin the keys o Bennachie
> Aneath a rash buss
> I the backward o Tullos.[3]

The intervention of *cailleachs* or carlins, maidens and giants in the making of lochs, mountains, islands, whirlpools and wells can be attested in all parts of Scotland, animating the landscape through a crudely powerful personification which still resonates with the worship of nature and its embodiment in now unknown myth and rituals. The surviving stories in their folklore contexts are often humorous in character but the same mythic underlay also persists in material which is legendary or explicitly religious.

Scotland is exceptionally rich in Saints' stories and traditions, many of which have depended on very localised transmission for their survival, often in association with specific Church sites and landscape features. Fuller transmission of Saints' legends (*legend* comes from the Latin *legenda*, meaning 'things to be read') involved written records in the medieval period stretching from Adomnan's *Life of Columba* to Bishop William Elphinstone's *Aberdeen Breviary*. The Reformation and seventeenth-century Puritanism set their face against local tradition but, nonetheless, stories of the Saints survived either as folklore or in neglected literary sources.

The term 'Celtic Saints' is a confusing description in this context because Saints' stories survive from Scots, Irish, Pictish, Brythonic, Anglian and Norse cultural contexts, indicating the extent to which early Christianity was paving the way for the later emergence of a recognisable Scottish nation. A comprehensive survey of Scottish Saints must include Cuthbert as well as Columba, Ebba as well as Ethernan and Magnus as well as Maelrubha.[4]

One interesting example is the story of Thenew or St Enoch which has survived as a medieval Life as well as in a variety of place names and local traditions.[5] The suspect Arthurian genealogy peddled by Geoffrey of Monmouth is nonetheless significant in relating the British or Brythonic kingdoms of southern Scotland to 'the age of Arthur'. Thenew, according to Geoffrey, was the daughter of Loth, king of Lothian, and Anna, Arthur's sister. Another of her uncles was Urien, king of neighbouring Rheged to the east. Thenew's brothers were Gawain and Mordred and her cousin Owen or (Gaelicised) Ewen was heir to Rheged.[6]

Whatever her royal pedigree, the nub of the tale is that Thenew gets the new Christian religion and decides to be a virgin bride of Christ rather than be the betrothed of her royal cousin, Ewen. Ewen's efforts to persuade her otherwise lead to rape which has echoes, despite the toning down of the monastic authors, of an older barbaric assertion of male right. Thenew's commitment to her new spiritual individualism is, however, unwavering, despite her pregnancy.

Now the full rigours of tribal society are brought to bear. Spared death by stoning, Thenew is pushed off Loth's precipitous fortress at Traprain Law in a ritual chariot. The intent seems as much sacrificial as punitive but Thenew is miraculously preserved unharmed. Next, she is cast adrift from Aberlady in a coracle, followed in her tidal course by the plentiful fish which are never thereafter landed on Aberlady shore.

Drifting out to the May islands, Thenew is revived by a freshwater spring (later a site of pilgrimage) and then carried upriver to the beach at Culross. More dead than alive, she breathes life into the embers of a fisherman's shoreline fire and gives birth. There she is found by the monks of St Serf. Her child is raised as Kentigern or Mungo who grows up to become the wonder-working Apostle of the Brythons, while she fulfils her vocation as a holy anchorite and royal patron of the new faith.

Clearly Thenew's story reflects the medieval pattern of a sequence of wonders, demonstrating the holy prowess of the Saint. But Thenew's marvels are very unchurchlike and close to an older empathy between natural and spiritual powers. The casting down from Traprain Law is in the Maiden Craig tradition. Aberlady loses its natural fertility while Thenew is nourished by a spring and gives birth to a royal Celtic culture hero rather than a devout monk. The precise association with important landmarks such as The Law, the Isle of May and the River Forth invests the landscape with a mythic quality. Nature is more than just the backcloth to a pious biography. Mungo, royal son of Ewen of Rheged and spiritual offspring of Thenew, still has pride of place in the underbelly of Glasgow Cathedral where his shrine gives that city its origin legend, coat of arms and continuing spiritual identity.[7]

Despite the best efforts of successive Christian reformers, Catholic and Protestant, religion has proved a powerful force for narrative continuity in Scotland and, even when institutional structures are disrupted, local tradition and folklore sustain underlying connections. This can occur in surprising ways and none more unexpected than in the story of Robert Kirk, the seventeenth-century episcopal minister of Balqhidder and Aberfoyle.[8]

Robert Kirk was the minister of Balqhidder and then of Aberfoyle, both in southern Perthshire, at a time in the late seventeenth century when the post-Reformation Church of Scotland was Episcopal and when rural Perthshire was still thoroughly Highland and Gaelic speaking. Kirk succeeded his father as minister at Aberfoyle and among his scholarly accomplishments were a reworking of the Irish Bible for Gaelic speakers and the publication of a Gaelic Psalter. Sadly, some years before his translation to Aberfoyle in 1685, Robert Kirk's first wife, Isobel, died and was buried in the kirkyard of Balqhidder.

So far so good, a notable but unexceptional life. However, Robert Kirk was his father's seventh and youngest son, a position reputed in Gaelic tradition to confer special gifts. Kirk evidenced a keen interest in the psychic phenomena of Gaelic culture, such as second sight, and in 1691 he produced *The Secret Commonwealth of Elves, Fauns and Faeries*.[9] This treatise is motivated by an Enlightenment spirit of enquiry and classification, but eschews rationalistic materialism in accepting the reality of an alternative spiritual world while questioning popular superstition.

People with mysterious learning are often ascribed supernatural powers in folk tradition and elevated to magus status. An earlier example of this phenomenon in Scottish tradition is Michael Scott, the medieval scholar whose Europe-wide magus reputation led to his recasting as Michael Scott the Border Wizard. Highland Perthshire in Kirk's day was still immune to Presbyterian rationalism and steeped in traditional Celtic culture.

Balqhidder Church itself is built beside a preaching hill which was probably in turn located at an older sacred site overshadowed by the spectacular Ben More. It is associated with St Angus and a very old carved stone retained in the Church shows the outline of a man holding out a chalice. Even after Kirk's time the area typified the resistance of Highland culture to Lowland ways and Balqhidder was to provide Rob Roy McGregor and his wife with their burial place. Add to this background the fact that Robert Kirk had already been touched by death through the loss of his first wife and you have the natural ingredients of a remarkable tale.

In 1692 not long after completion of 'The Secret Commonwealth,' Robert Kirk was walking on a hill near Aberfoyle when he fell unconscious and, being taken for dead, was buried. However, after the funeral at Aberfoyle Church, Kirk appeared to a relation and commanded him to tell their mutual cousin, Grahame of Duchray, that he had in fact been taken prisoner in fairyland and that only one hope of escape remained. An infant son born to the minister's second wife after his death was soon to be baptised at which occasion, Kirk warned, he would appear. On his appearance, Kirk instructed, Duchray should throw a knife over his head and the saving virtue of iron (a traditional protection against fairy power) would restore him to the mortal world. When the appointed time of baptism came, Kirk did appear but, paralysed by fear and shock, Grahame of Duchray failed to cast his dirk and Robert Kirk was lost to human society.

The Robert Kirk story is interesting because it demonstrates how a historical figure and circumstances can be translated into folklore and legend, if the cultural contexts are favourable. I say contexts in the plural because the legend of Robert Kirk, the spiritual magus, has outlived the Gaelic speaking community of South Perthshire which originally perceived Kirk as a man who, through birth, psychic gift and personal tragedy, had knowledge of a collectively recognised otherworld. In the late twentieth century, a dramatic treatment of the Kirk legend, Netta Reid's *The Shepherd Beguiled*,[10] was a popular success with Scottish theatregoers and repeatedly revived by Theatre Alba.

However, the mythic underlay of landscape and legend is also at work in the Robert Kirk story. The hill on which the minister was walking at the time of his death/disappearance was a known *Dun Sidhe* or fairy hill. Scotland is liberally scattered with these features which are sometimes, but not always, associated with Bronze Age burials. These hills were liminal – thresholds or portals to the other spiritual realm, with its population of Gods (later cast as the fairy folk) and of the dead. Let Robert Kirk himself be our commentator:

> There be many Places called Faerie-hills, which the Mountain People think impious and dangerous to peel or discover, by taking Earth or Wood from them; superstitiously believing the Souls of their Predecessors to dwell there. And for that end (say they) a Mote or Mount was dedicate beside every Church-yard, to receive the Souls till their Adjacent Bodies arise, and so became as a Faerie-hill; they useing Bodies of Air when called abroad.[11]

The traffic between this other supernatural world, whether peopled by the fairies, the good folk or the people of peace on land or by the selkies or seal people at sea, is a constant of Scottish folklore. The stories invite comparison with myths of underworld descent and ascent which inform the tale of Orpheus in Greek culture, the Babylonian Epic of Gilgamesh or the Egyptian stories of Isis and Osiris. But the Scottish tales of fairy are distinguished by a common Celtic perception of the other world as mystically enchanting and alluring, yet fatally cruel and cold. Immortality is beautiful but heartless; psychic gifts are as much curse as blessing.

Thomas of Erceldoune or Thomas the Rhymer is the Scottish paradigm in this respect. Taken by the beautiful Queen of Fairy for seven years, Thomas is allowed to return with the gift of prophecy but he never escapes thralldom and is ultimately recalled by a white deer back to the Eildon Forest where, according to another tradition, he remains awaiting his release.[12] In a parallel case, Tam Lin is freed by the courage of his mortal lover evoking this response from the Fairy Queen.

But had I kenned, Tam-Lin, she says
What now this night I see
I wad hae taen out thy twa grey een
And put in twa een o tree.[13]

Before leaving the animated and personified landscape of Scotland, we should mention the less transcendent creatures and monsters which people folklore. In the Scottish context, these include the kelpies or waterhorses, the largely malevolent urisks and glaistigs of the Highlands, the brownies, the trows of the Northern Isles and the various serpents, worms and dragons encountered in Highlands, Lowlands and Northlands.[14] These too convey, in local contexts, a spirit of place and a sense of the supernatural but they also have other practical functions, as detailed by Alan Bruford:

> Faeries and other supernatural beings, as well as serving to express the awe and reverence felt for wild nature, had several functions which are shown in such stories: to act as a nemesis on rash wishes; to serve as bogeys to frighten children away from dangerous places or wandering after dark and discourage anyone from going too far into the hills alone; and above all to act as scapegoats for anything which inexplicably went wrong, especially illness.[15]

Folklore of this kind also interacted with human and natural history. St Serf, whom we previously encountered at Culross, slew a dragon over the Ochils at Dunning.[16] This conflict may represent the holy man overcoming some fierce spiritual opposition to the new faith or there may be an echo of intertribal conflict in which the Saint took sides in the interests of his more Christianised patrons. St Columba, according to a strong tradition within the Columban monastic family, encountered a man-slaying water monster in the Great Glen when he was en route to Inverness to seek the support of Bridei, High King of the northern Picts.[17] Was this another opportunity to display supernatural prowess on a prestige-building expedition or an encounter with a proto-Loch-Ness-monster which still lurks in those waters as an evolutionary throwback?

In the Northern Isles, the dragon or serpent becomes a stoorworm, famously conquered on one occasion by young Assipattle who is more folk hero than heroic knight.[18] The fire-breathing worm is linked in this and other Norse tales to volcanoes. At the other end of Scotland there is a cluster of worm or dragon stories associated with sites north and south of the English border. The Linton Worm, for example, had its lair below the Cheviots and came out to terrorise the surrounding countryside. Several local champions lost life and limb trying to dispose of the beast until the Somerville Laird of Lariston decided to use strategy instead of strong-arm tactics. Noticing that the worm tended to sleep in the open after a good meal with its mouth open, he devised a wheel of straw and pitch. Setting this firebrand alight, he put it on his lance and, charging downhill, thrust it into the monster's throat. The marks of the worm's writhing death agonies are still to be seen forming the Hill of Wormiston.[19]

As presented, this is clearly a legend of place which may have merged with a historical memory of a Viking intrusion or earlier marauders. However, the straw fire-wheel is a well-known seasonal ritual, suggesting that the land and control of its fertility may be the key issue.[20] The story also explains how the Somervilles came into possession of the land of Linton as a local rhyme affirms:

> The wode Laird of Laristone
> Slew the worm of Worme's Glen
> And wan all Linton parochine.[21]

The Somervilles are an entirely historical Anglo-Norman family whose landholdings later incorporated the Drum Estate, south of Edinburgh.[22] There, the Somerville emblem of a lance and wheel of fire is still evident in stone and plaster, while a carving at Linton Church depicts a knight in battle with a smoky monster. Traditional stories operate at a variety of levels to achieve different purposes and functions.

They cannot be surgically separated from our historical understanding without significant damage being done to both parties.

Notes

1. For an excellent summary of Bennachie lore and topography, see McConnachie, Alex Inkson [1890], *Bennachie* reprinted in the Aberdeenshire Classics series (1985), Aberdeen: James G. Bisset, with a foreword by the Bailies of Bennachie.
2. For a full account of this remarkable site and its early history, see Ferguson, Robert Menzies (1905), *Logie: A Parish History*, Paisley: Alexander Gardner, Vol. 1.
3. *Bennachie*, p. 17.
4. For a concise introduction to this vast topic, see Smith, Donald (1997), *Celtic Travellers*, Edinburgh: The Stationery Office.
5. See 'Fragment of the Life of S. Kentigern' in MacQueen, John (ed.) (undated), *A Selection of Scottish Lives of Saints*, Edinburgh: School of Scottish Studies.
6. Geoffrey of Monmouth, *The History of the Kings of Britain*, trans. Thorpe, Lewis (1966), London: Penguin Classics, p. 209 and p. 221.
7. See Duncan, A. A. M., 'St Kentigern at Glasgow Cathedral in the Twelfth Century' in Fawcett, Richard (ed.) (1998), *Medieval Art and Architecture in the Diocese of Glasgow*, British Association of Archaeology Conference Transactions XXIII. A visit to Glasgow Cathedral can still evoke the centrality of Mungo's tomb to this remarkable medieval pilgrimage site.
8. See Kirk, Robert (1893), *The Secret Commonwealth of Elves, Fawns and Fairies*, ed. Andrew Lang, London: David Nutt.
9. Ibid.
10. Reid, Netta Blair (1986), *The Shepherd Beguiled*, Glasgow: Brown, Son & Ferguson.
11. *The Secret Commonwealth*, p. 79.
12. See Geddie, John (1920), *Thomas the Rymour*, Edinburgh: The Rymour's Club.
13. Kinsley, James (ed.) (1969), *The Oxford Book of Ballads*, Oxford: Oxford University Press, p. 20.
14. See, for example, McHardy, Stuart (1999), *Scotland: Myth, Legend and Folklore*, Edinburgh: Luath Press; MacDougall, James (1910), *Folktales and Fairy Lore*, Edinburgh: George Calder; Marwick, Ernest W. (1986), *The Folklore of Orkney*

and Shetland, London: Batsford; and Chambers, Robert (1826), *Popular Rhymes of Scotland*, Edinburgh: Chambers.

15. Bruford, Alan, 'Supernatural beliefs', in Daiches, David (ed.) (1993), *The New Companion to Scottish Culture*, Edinburgh: Polygon.
16. See 'The Life of Servanus', trans. Metcalfe, W. M. (1896), in *Ancient Lives of the Scottish Saints*, Edinburgh: Scottish Text Society.
17. Adomnan of Iona, *Life of St Columba*, trans. Sharpe, Richard (1995), London: Penguin Classics, pp. 175–6.
18. See Douglas, Sir George (ed.) (1892), *Scottish Fairy and Folk Tales*, London: W Scott, pp 58–73.
19. See Chambers, Robert (1842), *Popular Rhymes, Fireside Stories and Amusements of Scotland*, Edinburgh: Chambers, pp. 296–301.
20. See Hutton, Ronald (1996), *The Stations of the Sun*, Oxford: Oxford University Press, p. 311.
21. *Popular Rhymes of Scotland*, p. 296.
22. Ibid. pp. 297–301.

History Makers

———◆———

Historians are like storytellers inasmuch as they hand on and construct narratives. Historical narratives, however, are supposed to be based on diligent scrutiny of documentary and other forms of evidence. Of course, having assembled a mass of evidence, the historian must select the most significant elements and connect them in some form of causal or relational pattern, expressed primarily through narrative. In pursuing these ends, historians often use the materials and the techniques of oral storytelling.

History makers, though, often differ from storytellers in their ambition to create an overall master narrative within which the individual or separate stories of particular people and events are contained. This overarching dimension of the historian's art is more akin to the embracing vision of an epic poet than a teller of tales, and reveals a dominant bias or mode of interpretation in the historical work which is not so readily seen in the writer's detailed treatment of each area or period. The Jewish Scriptures, known to Christianity as The Old Testament, provided an early and very influential model of a master narrative. Then, in The New Testament, St Paul wrestled with the construction of a new master narrative, replacing the story of God's Chosen People with a drama of universal salvation through The Christ or Messiah. St Augustine of Hippo linked Paul's master narrative to the Roman Church and the fading Empire, in a way that was to shape historical thinking in the Christian West for centuries to come.[1]

Among the smaller medieval kingdoms of the Christian West was Scotland and, in common with other emergent nations, not least those overshadowed by more powerful neighbours, the Scots felt a need to explain the origins of their nationhood. The purpose of this search was to establish the identity of the Scots and to vindicate their independent existence, rather than the disinterested pursuit of knowledge. To this extent, the task was close to the function of the poet or storyteller, so it is no surprise that the ready materials were a compound of myth and legend.[2]

The problem was that the origins of the Scots were by no means clear and the issues involved have continued to fascinate and perplex historians to the present day. A variety of cultural groups, including Irish Scots, Picts, Celtic Britons or Brythons, Anglo-Saxons and Norse peoples were settled within the borders of the country now known as Scotland and all of them had, to some degree, shaped the history of that territory up to the twelfth century. To what extent did each of these and any other possible groups represent an 'indigenous' population and to what extent were they invaders or migrants? What were the dividing lines between the groups and how had they changed and when? The medieval solution to these issues was eminently practical and an instructive warning to all later history makers. The strongest institution in Scotland was kingship so the story, and therefore identity, of the nation was tied to the royal line of the Dalriadic Scots, which had united the Scots and Picts under Kenneth mac Alpin around 843; subsequently absorbed the British, Celtic or Brythonic kingdom of Strathclyde; pushed back the English frontier to the Tweed; and gradually reduced the political influence of the distant king of Norway. This solution involved a major simplification, not to say distortion, of Scotland's story but the medieval account of Scottish kingship was so successful that the testimonies of Brythonic poets, Anglo-Saxon chroniclers, Norse saga makers and local storytellers were sidelined.

Another reason for the effectiveness of the Scots kingship solution was the cultural prestige and quality of the Irish tradition which it accessed. The *Leabor Gabála* or *Book of Invasions* was an already existing, early medieval attempt by Irish monks to reconcile the biblical account of humanity with Irish myth and legend. It tells of a series of invasions and migrations culminating in the arrival of the Gaels or Milesians. According to the *Leabor Gabála* the Gaels replaced the language and traditions of earlier Irish peoples, including the ancestors of the Scots of Dalriada, with their own Q-Celtic speech. The Gaels are thus the common source of the Irish and Scots peoples and of the Irish and Gaelic languages.[3]

The story related by the *Leabor Gabála* makes the eponymous Gaedel Glas (later Latinised as Gathelus) a descendent, through Fenius the Scythian, of Noah. This Fenius had conveniently and impressively mastered all the languages of Babel and his son Nel or Neolus prospered in Egypt where he married Scota, Pharaoh's daughter. Nel, however, suffered a reverse when his father-in-law was drowned in the Red Sea in pursuit of the Israelites. Seen as an Israelite sympathiser, Nel and his son Gaedel Glas had to flee Egypt wandering round the Mediterranean till they settled in Spain, from where their descendent Mil led his Milesians or Gaels to Ireland.

The Scottish leg of this epic wandering was supplied by Gaelic oral tradition. The poem 'Duan Albanach', which was written down and expanded in the eleventh century, lists the invasions of Scotland or Alba by first the British Celts, then the Picts and then the Gaels.[4] The Gaelic invaders are specified as the descendants of 'Conaire the Gentle One', namely the three sons of Erc-Loarn, Fergus and Aonghus. Then the 'Duan' lists the Gaelic kings of Scotland in an asserted continuous succession from Fergus mac Eirc through Kenneth mac Alpin down to Malcolm III, or Canmore, the reigning monarch.

In combination with the Irish-Scots origin myth of the *Leabor Gabála,* which the poet presumes rather than repeats, the 'Duan Albanach' provides the Scottish kingdom with a lineage every bit as impressive as that of the English. They traced their royal origins from the invasion of the whole of Britain by Albanus, nephew of Brutus the Roman, through Arthur to the medieval kings. The English or British origin legend, which is fully developed in Geoffrey of Monmouth's *History of the Kings of Britain*, implies a claim to the whole of

Britain including Scotland.[5] Clearly a further reason for the success of the Scottish origin legend is its capacity to counter Geoffrey's claims on behalf of England's, by now, Anglo-Norman monarchy, with the even lengthier genealogy of the Scottish kings.

The makers of this account of the Scottish kingdom employed myth and legend, oral tradition and written records without distinction, to meet a pressing political and cultural need in the same ways as storytellers' creations are dictated by function and appeal. Moreover, the legend was developed and then reinforced by both written and oral means. In his seventh-century *Life of Columba*, Adomnan parallels the method of the *Leabor Gabála*'s anonymous authors when he anachronistically describes Columba an-ointing Aedan mac Gabrain as King of Dalriada, just as the prophet Samuel had anointed David King of Israel.[6] Though this story became a popular tradition, it clearly has a literary antecedent.

By contrast, in a later account by Walter Bower of a Scottish crowning – that of Alexander II at Scone in 1249 – the role of oral tradition is specifically emphasised:

In accordance with the custom which had grown up in antiquity right up to that time, after the solemn ceremony of the King's coronation the bishops with the earls brought the king to the Cross which stands in the cemetery on the east side of the Church . . . so when the king was solemnly seated on his royal seat of stone . . . there suddenly ap-peared a venerable, grey-haired figure, an elderly Scot. Though a wild Highlander he was honourably attired after his own fashion, clad in a scarlet robe. Bending his knee in a scrupulously correct manner and inclining his head, he greeted the king in his mother tongue, saying courteously: 'God Bless the King of Albany, Alexander mac Alexander, mac William, mac Henry, mac David . . .'[7]

The Gaelic Seanchaidh, or tradition bearer, then goes on to recite the complete genealogy of the Scottish kings right back to Gaythelos, Neolus or Nel and Scota, daughter of the

Pharoah of Egypt. When the Scots had to plead their case against Edward I of England's claim to Scotland at the Papal Court in Rome in 1301, they used the same traditional genealogy and the origin legend which it perpetuated as a legal defence of Scottish independence. These traditional arguments are again deployed in the resonant Declaration of Arbroath in 1320 but, despite this repetition, the legend, as opposed to the genealogy, never gained popular oral currency as a story since it lacks vivid characters or an embodied setting. The origin legend smacks of academic construction and no-one now cares about Gaedel Glas or Scota. You cannot legislate for a story's survival.

The Scottish origin legend is uncritically absorbed into the monumental work of Walter Bower, the Abbot of Inchcolm, in the fifteenth century. In this regard Bower follows the lead of Andrew of Wyntoun, the prior at Loch Leven, whose *Oryginale Cronykil*, completed in the 1420s in Scots verse, locates the history of Scotland within a scheme of universal sacred history beginning with the Creation.[8] But Bower's *Scotichronicon* builds more extensively on the fourteenth-century work of another clerical chronicler, John of Fordun, a chantry priest of St Machar's Cathedral in Aberdeen. Like Fordun before him, Bower was a genuine enquirer and collector of sources, concerned to provide for Scotland a national history or, as Fordun describes it, a 'Chronicle of the Scottish Nation' written in Latin, the language of classical scholarship and religious legitimacy.[9] The reason for this activity is not hard to see since, despite the best efforts of William Wallace and Robert the Bruce, the fourteenth century had brought extended war and repeated English invasions: the identity and survival of the Scottish nation remained in doubt. A century later, as Bower took up his pen, the assassination of James I had ended a brief period of stability and progress, throwing everything once more into doubt.

It is hard to underestimate the importance of the *Scotichronicon* since its overall structure established a master narrative which subsequent generations have amended but never wholly supplanted. Equally, Bower's chronicle is packed with vivid storytelling detail which has lived on in the popular imagination and shaped Scotland's sense of itself, even when the Abbot of Inchcolm has been forgotten. This is at least partly because Bower has drawn on many oral sources as well as the more austere work of Fordun, his clerical predecessor.

In creating his sixteen volumes of material, enlarged from Fordun's five, Walter Bower pursues many interests. He is a preacher with a keen eye for moral examples and pious warnings, influenced in form and tone by the preaching manuals of medieval Christendom. He is also an enthusiastic gatherer of traditions with a weakness for the vivid tale. But, above all, he is a Scottish churchman, concerned to vindicate the religious destiny of the Scottish nation. 'Christ! He is not a Scot,' asserts Bower, with a final flourish, 'who is not pleased with this book.'

To the origin legend of the *Leabor Gabála* and the genealogy of the 'Duan Albanach', Bower adds effective colour with the legend of the Stone of Destiny (brought to Ireland from Spain by Simon Breac) as a talisman of Scottish kingship, the translation of the bones of St Andrew from Greece to Scotland by St Regulus, the sign of the cross in the sky at the Battle of Athelstaneford and many other stories reflecting divine guidance and succour for a struggling nation. It is Bower who lays down the main lines of the story of Macbeth as we know it, ignoring testimony to Macbeth as a legitimate and successful Celtic ruler in favour of Macbeth the murderer and tyrant, for the Abbot is strongly committed to the Stewart line as the guarantor of Scottish kingship and so, in turn, of Church and Nation.[10]

Bower is also enthusiastic about the marriage of Malcolm III and the devout Queen Margaret which brings his two favourite causes, the Scottish crown and religious orthodoxy, into close alliance. To the main narrative, laid out by Margaret's own confessor, Turgot, in his 'Life of St Margaret',[11] Bower adds a legend from local tradition describing how, after her canonisation at Rome, the monks of Dunfermline tried to move Margaret's coffin to a shrine behind the high altar. The coffin could not be budged until Malcolm's body was 'raised and honoured in the same way'.[12]

This incident in turn paves the way for Sir John of Wemyss's vision of Margaret on the eve of the battle of Largs:

> He appeared to be standing at the [north] doorway of the church at Dunfermline. A lady of radiant beauty and resplendent in full royal attire came quickly out of the aforesaid church. She was leading on her right arm a distinguished-looking knight, clad in gleaming armour, girded with the sword of a knight and wearing a helmet with a crown on it. Three noble knights, brisk and cheerful in appearance, followed them at a stately pace and in due order, all gleaming in similar armour. The knight was not a little disturbed by the suddenness of this unexpected encounter, but took comfort from the beauty and benevolence of the lady who headed the group, and so addressed the sainted queen as follows: 'Glorious lady, please tell me who you are and where you and your noble companions are going.' She replied: 'I am Margaret, formerly queen of Scots. The knight who has my arm is the lord king Malcolm my husband, and these knights who are following us are our sons, the most renowned kings of this realm while they lived. In company with them I am hurrying to defend our country at Largs and to win a victory over the usurper who is unjustly trying to make my kingdom subject to his rule. For you must know that I received this kingdom from God, granted in trust to me and to our heirs for ever.' When the queen finished speaking she quickly disappeared and the knight awoke.[13]

Bower's tone and imagery here borrow directly from the conventions of medieval Romance, but the application to Scotland is clever, with the royal line of Margaret and Malcolm brought together in one image. Soon afterwards, as Sir John of Wemyss is praying by Margaret's shrine, news of the victory arrives and he is cured of chronic illness. This victory secures the integrity of the Scottish kingdom against Norwegian power but, faced with a paucity of real information about the battle, Bower has elaborated a pious anecdote into a full-blown tale of divine and miraculous intervention. Modern historians have been no more effective in establishing what really happened at Largs but less imaginative.

The most influential section of the *Scotichronicon* is Bower's account based on Fordun of the Wars of Independence. This is a saga with two heroes, the popular Laird and Guardian of Scotland, William Wallace, and the ruthless but heroic nobleman, Robert the Bruce. Although, by the time of writing, Barbour's heroic poem *The Bruce* was already in circulation, Bower, elaborating on Fordun, shaped the saga of Wallace and was the first to provide the combined narrative. In a typical storytelling touch, Bower has Wallace and Bruce meet after the battle of Falkirk, at which Bruce had fought on the winning side with the English. Wallace reproaches Bruce for not taking up his natural role as a leader of the Scottish nation, so leaving the commoner Wallace to fight for independence: Robert, Robert, it is your inactivity and womanish cowardice that spur me to the liberation of the native land that is legally yours.[14] This little sermon, according to the Abbot, sank home, leading eventually to Bruce's conversion to the cause as 'God raised up another saviour for the Scottish Nation', albeit one inconveniently capable of murdering his Comyn rival in front of a Christian altar.

The trials, tribulations and occasional triumphs of the Scottish nation, focused through Scotland's kings and queens and drawing on folk tradition, poetry and religion, rapidly became the backbone of Scottish historical and cultural identity. Fordun, Andrew Wyntoun and Bower were followed, with varying degrees of historical analysis and accuracy, by Blind Hary (in Scots verse), Hector Boece (in Latin prose, translated by John Bellenden), Lindsay of Pitscottie (in Scots prose), George Buchanan (in Latin prose) and other successors on a smaller or larger scale, up to and including Sir Walter Scott in the nineteenth century. Of course these authors wrote from very different religious and philosophical perspectives. George Buchanan is much more concerned with historical evidence than, say, Hector Boece though both were scholarly Humanists, albeit divided by the Reformation and religion. Scott, as we shall see, seeks to incorporate the older material in a new master narrative which takes account of the Union of the Parliaments in 1707 and the Enlightenment. But none escapes the influence of Bower.

There is, nonetheless, a distinct shift in tone from the fifteenth-century chroniclers, with whom Boece still identifies, to the sixteenth-century historians. In the introduction to the *Book of Pluscardin*, probably compiled at the monastery by Maurice Buchanan, the editor writes:

> Although good Chronicles and Gestes are in favour and please many hearers, yet men, whose attention is occupied by the many pressing duties as well as the ever-present and varied cares of life, cannot without great difficulty give their time to the perusal of heavy tomes – a labour which oftimes makes them weary and deadens in their hearts the desire to learn. It is therefore our intention under correction of those whom it concerns or may in any way in time coming concern, to treat briefly and concisely of every matter which is useful and profitable; and, as it is vanity to do by more words what may be done by fewer, to seek out, extract, and arrange, like a honey-bee amid wild flowers, doing them no hurt, whatever seems necessary for the proper telling of the story.[15]

The chronicler is engaged and interested but also to some extent removed from events, selecting and arranging his material with a combination of editorial discipline and storytelling delight. Even when the chronicler is more partisan and passionate – as Bower often is – there is a distance of time which allows the master narrative or arrangement to take shape.

We see this perspective come unstuck in Bower's own pages in a very emotional way. When he arrives chronologically at the recent murder of his royal patron James I in 1437, the Abbot can barely continue his narrative:

> This fateful year then smote this famous kingdom and greatly shook it. It was my plan to put off my account of

the manner and way of it, because it is not something that I want to write about. But now [after more mature thought] two considerations rouse me to write. On the one hand the exceptional nature of his [that is, the king's] virtues of natural endowment and character compels me to speak; and on the other hand I am reduced to tears by the harm which the community has suffered. Now therefore I am forced to unfold a gloomy account although it is much against my inclination. But because the human condition must pay its debts to death, but bitter death does not spare that human condition, encompassing the classes of individuals and the single examples of classes which live in the flesh under its law, see how his mortal fate brought our king to the end of his reign and, anticipating before its allotted time the date when this slight payment was due, if God had bestowed anything on him, removed that which was due! I think therefore that there is truth in the sentiment of the saying: suddenly when it is not expected, misfortune occurs, disaster intrudes, illness strikes, death which no one escapes cuts life short.[16]

The pressure of present events has become too great and Bower proceeds with a very perfunctory account of the king's death, supplemented by a rhetorical eulogy of his kingly and personal virtues.

Contrast Bower's treatment of events with the anonymous account, dating from soon after the murder, which was translated from a lost Latin version by the English scribe and editor, John Shirley:

The King that same time standing in his nightgown, all unclothed save his shirt, his cap, his comb, his kerchief, his furred pinsons, upon the form and the foot-sheet, so standing afore the chimney, playing with the Queen and other ladies and gentlewomen with her, cast off his nightgown for to have gone to bed. But he harkened and heard great noise without and great clattering of harness, and men armed, with great sight of torches. Then he remembered him and imagined anon that it should be the false traitorous knight, his deadly enemy, Sir Robert Graham: and suddenly the Queen, with all the other ladies and gentlemen, ran to the chamber door and found it open; and they would have shut it but the locks were so blundered that they neither could nor might shut it. The King prayed them to keep the said door as well as they might and he would do all his might to keep him to withstand the false malice of his traitors and enemies, he supposing to have brasten the farments of the chamber windows, but they were so square and so strongly soldered in the stones with molten lead thay they might not be brasten for him without more and stronger help. For which cause he was ugly astonished, and in his mind could think on no other succour but start to the chimney and take the tongs of iron that men righted the fire with in time of need, and under his feet he mightily brast up a plank of the chamber floor and therewithal covered him again and entered low down among the ordure of the privy, that was all of hard stone and none window nor issue thereupon save a little square hole even at the side of the bottom of the privy, that at the making thereof of old time was left open to cleanse and ferme the said privy, by the which the King might well have escaped, but he made to let stop it well three days afore, hard with stone, because that when he played there at the paume the balls that he played with oft ran in at that foul hole, for there was ordained a fair playing place for the King.[17]

This narrative clearly draws on a vivid eyewitness account. The physical detail is immediate and not necessarily pleasant. There is a strong sense of drama, underpinned by ironic perceptions which link the circumstances and the underlying significance assigned by the authorial voice. Here is the King, covered in human faeces, beneath his own gracious tennis court. The impact of this assassination was considerable with each writer and storyteller adding their own touches. Hector Boece, for example, is the first to record how Kate 'Bar-the-Door' or 'Bar-Lass' uses her own arm in place of the missing bolt, but in vain.

The narrative is driven on by a growing tension between

the violence of the hunt and the fear of the quarry and the denouement is desperate and brutal:

> Therewithal one of the said tyrants and traitors, cleped Sir John Hall, descended down to the King with a great knife in his hand and the King, doubting him sore of his life, caught him mightily by the shoulders and with full great violence cast him under his feet, for the King was of his person and nature right manly strong. And another of Hall's brethren seeing that the King had the better of him, went down also for to destroy the King: and anon as he was there descended the King caught him manly by the neck and cast him above that other, and so he defouled them both under him that all a long month after men might see how strongly the King had holden them by the throats, and greatly the King struggled with them for to have bereaved them of their knives, by the which labour his hands were all for cut. But an the King had been in any wise armed, he might well have escaped this matter by the length of his fighting with those two false traitors; for if the King might any while longer have saved himself, his servants and much other people of the town by some fortune should have had some knowledge thereof and so have come to his succour with help. But alas the while, it will not be. Fortune was to him adverse as in preserving his life any longer.
>
> Therewithal that odious and false traitor Sir Robert Graham, seeing the King laboured so sore with those two false traitors which he had cast under his feet, and that he waxed faint and was weary, and that he was weaponless, the more pity was, descended down also unto the King, with an horrible and mortal weapon in his hand. And then the King cried him mercy. 'Thou cruel tyrant,' quoth Graham to him. 'Thou hadst never mercy of lords born of thy blood, ne of none other gentlemen that came in they danger, therefore no mercy shalt thou have here.' Then said the King, 'I beseech thee that for the salvation of my soul, ye will let me have a confession.' Quoth the said Graham, 'Thou shalt never have other confessor but this same sword.' And therewithal he smote him through the body and therewithal the good King fell down.[18]

28

This is not disinterested or dispassionate storytelling; it has been argued that the intent is to describe the death of an allegedly tyrannous ruler as a warning to English rulers. However, it prefigures a new kind of historical writing in which the pressure of the present is uppermost, and the dramatic psychology of the tale is intended to strike with immediate force – storytelling and history merge with journalism. This tone is taken up in Scotland by Lindsay of Pitscottie in his *Chronicles of Scotland*, written in the 1530s,[19] and by John Knox in his *History of the Reformation in Scotland* which was composed in the 1560s.[20]

With events such as the merciless assassination of James I in the Blackfriars Monastery at Perth, Scottish history-making moved decisively out of the cloister. Such bloody events had happened before but, in future, writers and storytellers would be required to keep pace with an ever-present succession of dramatic conflicts.

Notes

1. See Cupitt, Don (1991), *What is a Story?*, London: SCM Press, pp. 62–3 and 114–7.
2. The following account is indebted to Ferguson, William (1998), whose *The Identity of the Scottish Nation: An Historic Quest*, Edinburgh: Edinburgh University Press, provides an unsurpassed account of the Scots origin myths and their significance.
3. For a full account of the *Leabor Gabála* Erenn, see Ibid. pp. 3–21.
4. For the full text and translation of the poem, see Jackson, Kenneth, 'The Duan Albanach' in *Scottish Historical Review* (1957), pp. 125–37.
5. See Geoffrey of Monmouth, *The History of the Kings of Britain*, trans. Thorpe, Lewis (1966), London: Penguin Classics.
6. See Adomnan of Iona, *Life of St Columba*, trans. Sharpe, Richard (1995), London: Penguin Classics, pp. 208–9 and 355–6.
7. Bower, Walter, *Scotichronicon*, Vol. 5, Books IX and X, ed. Taylor, Simon and Watt, D. E. R., with Scott, Brian (1990), Aberdeen: Aberdeen University Press, pp. 292–5.
8. See Amours, F. J. (ed.) (1902–14), *The Original Chronicle of Andrew of Wyntoun*, Edinburgh: Scottish Text Society.

9. For a general introduction to the content and ethos of Bower's monumental work, see Bower, Walter, *A History Book for Scots: Selections from Scotichronicon*, ed. D. E. R. Watt (1998), Edinburgh: Mercat Press. For the foundations laid by Fordun, see Johannis de Fordun, *Chronica Gentis Scotorum*, ed. William F. Skene (1871), Edinburgh: Edmonston and Douglas.

10. Ibid.

11. See Turgot 'The Life of St Margaret Queen of Scotland' in *Ancient Lives of the Scottish Saints*, trans. Metcalfe, W. M. (1896), Edinburgh: Scottish Text Society. Andrew of Wyntoun's *Original Chronicle* also includes this tradition.

12. Bower, Walter, *Scotichronicon*, Vol. 5, Books IX and X, ed. Taylor, Simon and Watt, D. E. R., with Scott, Brian (1990), Aberdeen: Aberdeen University Press, pp. 296–9.

13. Ibid. pp. 326–39.

14. Bower, Walter *Scotichronicon*, Vol. 6, Books XI and XII ed. Shead, Norman F., Stevenson, Wendy B., and Watt, D. E. R., with Borthwick, Alan, Latham, R. E., Phillips, J. R. S. and the late Smith, Martin S. (1990), Aberdeen: Aberdeen University Press, pp. 95–9.

15. Skene, Felix J. H. (ed.) (1877), *Liber Pluscardensis*, Edinburgh: William Paterson, p. 3.

16. Bower, Walter, *Scotichronicon*, Vol. 8, Books XV and XVI ed. Watt, D. E. R. (1990), Aberdeen: Aberdeen University Press, pp. 300–1.

17. See 'The Dethe of the Kynge of Scotis' in Stevenson, Joseph (ed.), *The Life and Death of James the First of Scotland*, Edinburgh: The Maitland Club, p. 55.

18. Ibid. pp. 55–59

19. See Robert Lindsay of Pitscottie *Historie and Cronicles of Scotland* Vols I and II, ed. A. E. T. G. Mackay (1894), Edinburgh: William Blackwood and Sons.

20. See Knox, John, *The History of the Reformation of Religion in Scotland*, ed. Cuthbert Lennox (1905), London: Andrew Melrose.

Gaelic and Highland Traditions

◆

Discussion so far has emphasised Scotland's oral traditions in the plural and the cultural diversity of a nation which was made up from Irish-Scottish, British, Pictish, Anglian and Norse components. However, the oldest continuous tradition of oral storytelling in Scotland is Gaelic, deriving from the centuries when the Gaelic world embraced Ireland and western Scotland without cultural distinction. This period may stretch back into prehistory but can only be measured linguistically and historically from the colonisation of Argyll from Ulster in the fourth century until the break-up of Gaelic aristocratic society, first in Ireland and then in Scotland in the seventeenth and eighteenth centuries. Nonetheless, elements of this oral culture survived in Scotland into the late twentieth century, long enough to become the focus of conscious preservation and revival.

Gaelic oral tradition is a many-layered creation which was accumulated and enriched over a long period of time and it bears comparison with the finest traditions of song, music and story in world culture. It has also been instrumental in the shaping of Scottish culture though, for reasons which we will touch on later, Scots have often peddled a distorted view of the Highlands and Gaelic society. Due to the unification of Scotland under Gaelic kingship, Irish/Scottish influence spread throughout Scotland in the medieval period. Politically, linguistically, geographically and culturally Gaelic tradition is integral to the making of the Scottish Kingdom and to the survival of a distinct Scottish identity. It is, therefore, surprising that the riches of Gaelic storytelling are not better known in Scotland as a whole, even in translation, and more widely acknowledged within the current storytelling revival.

In the common Irish/Scottish world of Gaelic culture, storytellers classified their tales by type, according to their subject matter. The categories about which we have information include Destructions, Cattle Raids, Courtships, Cave Stories, Battles, Feasts, Voyages, Tragic Deaths, Adventures, Elopements, Slaughters, Irruptions, Visions, Sieges, Conceptions and Births, Frenzies, Loves, Expeditions and Invasions.[1] These categories apply regardless of whether the material might be classed as history or legend, myth or dream – the story was the thing.

Although Gaelic oral tradition was learned and sustained by orders of poets, genealogists and druids who enjoyed aristocratic patronage, the storytelling categories are not a Celtic equivalent of the folk tale types and motifs applied so enthusiastically by modern scholars.[2] The story types listed above related in a very practical way to particular occasions and audiences. A Birth Story might appropriately welcome a new child but Tragic Deaths were not the stuff of wedding feasts. This accords with the practice of storytellers, then and since, and would influence both the selection and the combination of stories within a particular event, though Gaelic storytellers would probably function over a number of days rarely offering more than one lengthy tale on any single occasion.

The categorisation of Adventures, Elopements and so forth mirrors a very conservative tribal society in which most occasions, and therefore many stories, would bear some kind of ritual significance. The recital of the story would convey psychological, spiritual and even magical benefit at the start of a hunt, a voyage or a war, at rites of passage or at seasonal festivals. However, the categories are also artistically shrewd and a much better way for a storyteller to select the mood and effect of a story than a structural analysis of types (for example, stories of lame heroes) which bears no relationship to audience or occasion. Unfortunately, it is not always clear to which categories particular stories apply and many more stories have been lost. Nonetheless, it is always worth pondering the Celtic tale types in relation to any individual Scottish Gaelic tale from the older layers of tradition.

Gaelic stories are more conventionally classified by scholars according to the manuscript collections made by monks and, later, native scribes. The oddly named Historical Cycles refer to the Ulster and Fenian Cycles revolving around the unhistorical heroes of Ulster, principally Cuchulain and the Fian or Fenians led by Fionn Mac Cuill. There is a Mythological Cycle of tales mainly preserved in Ireland and then a wealth of Hero Tales and Romances common, like the Historical Cycles, to Ireland and Scotland. As folk traditions intermingled with and then, to some extent, superseded the classical Hero Tales, stories of the supernatural, legends of place, clan stories, historical tales and humorous anecdotes all asserted their place within the common cultural stream. In exploring these story kinds, an impression can be gained of the sources still available to Scottish storytelling as a whole from Gaelic tradition.

The Ulster Cycle finds its fullest expression in *The Tain*, or *Cattle Raid*, which reflects an Iron Age warrior aristocracy battling over specifically Irish terrain.[3] However, *The Tain* is wrapped round with other tales including an important sequence of pre-stories in which Scottish connections come to the fore. 'The Tragic Death of the Sons of Uisneach' involves exile in Scotland from where Naoise and his brothers are recalled to a treacherous death, leading in turn to the suicide of the tragic heroine Deirdre. This story was popular in Scotland as well as Ireland and it has both a Scottish manuscript and oral tradition.[4] These Irish/Scottish connections predate the colonisation of Argyll as is shown by the story of how Cuchulain, hero of *The Tain*, comes to be trained by the warrior queen Sgathach, whom tradition has located in Skye. Here Cuchulain fights with and then mates with variously Sgathach's daughter Uathach, another Amazon Aife, or Sgathach herself, before returning to Ulster. A sequel tale relates how Aife gives birth to a son, Conlaoch, who grows up and travels to Ulster where he challenges the warriors of Conchobar the king, whose principal champion then slays the upstart. The champion is Cuchulain, the boy's father. This sequel forms the subject of a heroic ballad which was widely sung in Scotland, while Cuchulain's training with Sgathach and the birth of Conlaoch are well-represented in oral tradition, not least in Skye and Uist.[5]

If the Ulster tales have Scottish connections, the Fenian Cycle has been thoroughly transplanted to Scotland and indigenised over many centuries. Fionn and the Fian are no more historical than Cuchulain and the Ulster warriors, since both cycles clearly concern culture heroes with magical and semi-divine powers. Nonetheless, there is an entirely different quality to the tales of Fionn. The tribal warriors of *The Tain* are tied to their territory and fated to defend it to the death – and death in battle is the inevitable and proper closure for a heroic biography. The Fenian warriors are a roving band, required to undertake defensive duties but free to live off the land by hunting. There is still death and violence aplenty but it is a more carefree world in which the ordeals of magical encounters, battles, loves, disputes and trickery are normally overcome. Fionn's warrior band includes stooges as well as straight men and there are explicitly humorous episodes, as well as darker passages such as Fionn's complicity in the death of the unbearably handsome Diarmaid. To be a Fian is essentially to step outside the ties of tribe and kin and to undertake special initiations into skills of hunting, fighting, music and poetry.

Nature is an important player in the Fenian stories, providing their context and imagery. According to Irish tradition, there was to be a division of Ireland between the two sons of Feradach Fechtnach, the king. Tuathal took the treasure hoards, the cattle, the raths and the settlements, but Fiacha, progenitor of the Fian, took the rocks and estuaries, fruits, fish and game. The share which the aristocracy thought worst was the one preferred by the warrior band. As Myles Dillon puts it, 'the life of wild nature is the choice of the Fian'.[6]

The emphasis on a natural setting, as opposed to the forts, fords and settlements of *The Tain*, allows the Fenian stories to be easily transferred to new areas, and key incidents in the Cycle, such as the death of Diarmaid, are claimed by several places in Scotland. The twelfth-century *Acallam na Senorach*, or *Colloquy of the Old Men*, an Irish compendium of Fenian stories, explicitly celebrates nature – Irish and Scottish:

34

Patrick said again: 'Well, Cailte, my soul, what was the best hunting that the Fenians ever had in Ireland or in Scotland?' 'The hunting of Arran,' said Cailte. 'Where is that?' said Patrick. 'Between Scotland and Pictland,' said Cailte, 'and we used to go there with three companies of the fianna on Lammas Day, and we would get plenty of hunting there until the cuckoo called from the treetops in Ireland. And sweeter it was than any music to hear the cry of the birds there, as they rose from the waves and coasts of the island. Thrice fifty flocks of birds frequented it, of every colour, blue and green and grey and yellow.' And Cailte sang a lay:

Arran of the many stags
The sea strikes against its shoulder
Isle where companies are fed,
Ridge on which blue spears are reddened.
Skittish deer are on her peaks,
Delicious berries on her manes,
Cool waters in her rivers,
Mast upon her dun oaks.
Greyhounds are there and beagles,
Blackberries and sloes of the dark blackthorn,
Her dwellings close against the woods,
Deer scattered about her oak-woods.

Gleaning of purple upon her rocks,
Faultless grass upon her slopes,
Over her fair shapely crags
Noise of dappled fawns a-skipping.
Smooth is her level land, fat are her swine,
Bright are her fields,
Her nuts upon the tops of her hazel-wood,
Long galleys sailing past her.
Delightful it is when the fair season comes;
Trout under the brinks of her rivers,
Seagulls answer each other round her white cliff,
Delightful at all times is Arran!
[trans. Kuno Meyer]⁷

This quotation highlights the combination of song and story which is typical of Fenian lore. Tales of Fionn are preserved in Scotland as ballads or heroic lays, as prose tales and as both in combination.[8] This makes the Fenian Cycle an exceptionally rich resource for the storyteller, traditional or contemporary, since the two media in conjunction offer a wider narrative and emotional range than either would in isolation. The ballads and stories may owe their transmission partially to separate manuscript traditions, but the oral tradition has happily combined the two through the agency of versatile performers capable of exploiting the dual potential. In Scotland, even more than in Ireland, the Fenian tales owe their survival to the vigorous and widespread devotion of folk artists of the highest calibre. To this extent, the instinct of James Macpherson, deviser of the Ossian poems, that the Fenian Cycle is the closest Scotland comes to a native epic tradition was correct, though, as we shall see, he seems to have profoundly misunderstood or misrepresented the nature of that tradition and its folk roots.

In the 1950s, John Lorne Campbell and Calum MacLean recorded a still impressive cycle of Fenian tales from Angus MacLellan in South Uist, beginning with the birth of Fionn and his getting of wisdom when he unknowingly burns himself on the salmon of wisdom and then sucks his thumb.[9] These stories represented a relatively small proportion of Angus's extensive repertoire and had given way in popularity to shorter, simpler folk tales. But, interestingly, he had learnt the stories as a young man from a single older tradition bearer, showing how easily oral tradition can close a gap of centuries. As late as the nineteenth century, while many storytellers would have a version of the most popular items, such as 'Diarmaid and Grainne', some may have been known for their particular attachment to the tales and ballads of Fionn. Angus MacLellan's cycle also incorporates the 'Ballad of the Smithy' which concerns the retempering of Fionn's sword Mac a'Luin, while his 'Death of Diarmaid' is essentially a ballad expanded with a prose addition.

A final important difference between the Ulster and Fenian cycles is noteworthy. *The Tain* and its associated tales have a dramatic immediacy and force which places them in a historic present. The tales of Fionn imply a golden age which is past. This is not the world of a warrior epic but of conscious Romance and even sometimes of nostalgic long-ing. Fionn's son the poet Oisin lives on into old age, as a last representative of an era, and the Fenian ballads of Oisin are a lament for and celebration of what are viewed as ideal Gaelic virtues: love of hunting, delight in nature, physical prowess, beauty, loyalty and poetic skill. It is a fantasy world but set in a real landscape and imbued with genuine emo-tions. The teller of Fenian tales must be in love with imagination itself, as well as adept at the skills of folk narrative, for anything like the original effect within the Gaelic community to be recaptured.

If this is true of the Fenian Cycle, it is even more strongly applicable to the huge corpus of Gaelic Hero Tales and Romances which comprise one of the richest archives of oral folk tale worldwide. Like the stories of Fionn and his band, these lengthy tales have been transmitted to us through folk tale tellers but the stories themselves are the product of oral folk traditions and medieval manuscript reciters. When the gestes and chansons of medieval Romance were popular in the royal courts and aristocratic halls of Europe, the High-land lords and chiefs patronised their own kind of hero tale, packed with a distinctively Gaelic brand of marvel, magic and adventure in which God and knightly virtues do not figure. These tales sat easily alongside the Fenian stories and, like that cycle, they both borrowed from folk tale traditions and eventually, as the native aristocracy declined, passed back into the repertoire of local storytellers.[10]

We know a lot about these stories because of the indefa-tigable labours of nineteenth century Scottish Gaelic folk tale collectors, inspired and to a large extent organised by John Francis Campbell of Islay. Despite the publication of (to date) six volumes of *West Highland Tales*, a landmark volume of Fenian ballads, successor series such as Lord Archibald Campbell's *Waifs and Strays of Celtic Tradition* and translations from the *Dewar Manuscripts* of Inveraray Castle, much of the work of Campbell and his associates remains unedited and unpublished. Moreover, many of the translations presented in the original four volumes of *Popular Tales of the West Highlands* (1860–2) frustrate rather than assist the general reader, since they are intended to be a literal accompaniment to the Gaelic transcription of manuscripts, which in turn need extensive textual work if they are to yield up all their linguistic clues. The overall impression is of a kist of treasure which, as yet, has been only partially prised open.

A typical example of the Romance Tale is the story of Young Iain, son of the King of France.[11] France, however, does not figure in the tale any more than Greece, Lochlann (Norway) or Italy are real places in this genre which hooks its fantasy on to a superficial medieval geography. In fact, Iain's first encounter is with a Bodach, a supernatural male figure, against whom he throws dice. This proves a bad move from which Iain recovers only by beating the Bodach at wrestling. Now Iain has an ally and companion in the Bodach which is just as well because, next, he takes on a sorceress, the Great Cailleach, at cards and ends up under a spell. Fortunately, the Bodach, now named Black Toe, sets off on a journey to counter the spell with Iain mounted on a spirited filly and the Bodach racing along beside him. They reach an inn where they are waylaid by the attractions of the Queen of Lochlann but she has her own troubles, which, in typical Romance style, have to be resolved at length before Iain Og and Black Toe can continue on their own travels, which then take them to the palace of the King of Erin. After watching this duo slaughter three times five hundred of his best troops, the King of Erin decides, instead of fighting, to tell the new arrivals 'the story of my joys and my woe'. This is the beginning of a long in-tale, or story-within-a-story, involving the King and his sixteen foster brothers and a monstrous Bodach called the Dark Fellow. Nothing then, of course, will do except that Iain Og will go to the cave of Dark Fellow with Black Toe and the King of Erin. The next sequence mirrors the in-tale but reverses the outcome, as Iain cuts off Dark Fellow's head and brings the sixteen foster brothers back to life. The tale then appears to symmetrically unravel via the King of Erin's palace, the Queen of Loch-lann's attractions and the Old Cailleach. However, what appears to be a closure (surely Iain Og's powers are now equal to the sorceress?) is denied when the Cailleach puts the hero under another spell, so unleashing another set of adventures involving yet another Bodach who turns out to be Black Toe's brother. Finally, the Cailleach is defeated by a combination of guile and a decapitated head. The hero has exhibited foolhardiness and courage but, eventually, with Black Toe's help, his magic proves stronger than that of the sorceress.

What on earth is it all about? It is certainly meant to entertain rather than instruct and the labyrinthine plot, with its parallel turns that then deflect into another circuit, offers the same kind of aesthetic satisfaction/frustration as a maze. Along the way, the adventures are fantastic and rumbus-tious, with touches of sexual humour, slapstick or silent-movie-type action and a host of vivid folk tale motifs, often involving magical powers. There are also passages of tre-mendous linguistic exuberance, known as runs, which bub-ble with sometimes obscure energy. This, for example, is one of the old Cailleach's spells in literal translation:

> I lay thee under spells and crosses
> Under the nine cowfetters of the widely-roaming,
>   traveller-deluding fairy-woman
> That same sorry little wight more feeble and misguided than
>   myself
> Take thy head, thine ear and thy life's career from thee
> Unless thou find out for me
> All there is to know about the King Erin's joy and woe.[12]

'Young Iain, the Son of the King of France' adds up to a lot of mind-stretching fun involving linguistic skill, visual ima-gination, excellent memory and a talent to entertain. It is, therefore, worth noting that this tale was recorded from the oral recitation of a labourer in Glen Barra, called Roderick MacNeill, and that it was known by many crofters, fishermen and estate workers across the Highlands in the mid-nineteenth century, most of whom could not read or write. The same situation applies to the even more popular hero tale of 'Conall Gulban', which, in one version recorded from a labourer near Dunoon, stretched to sixty foolscap pages. Campbell's collectors gathered similar versions of this Romance in Uist, Barra, the Beauly Firth and Paisley and, in 1959, Calum Maclean of the School of Scottish Studies recorded a full version of the story from Angus MacLellan on South Uist.[13]

'Conall Gulban' is a more literary Romance than 'Iain Og' and clearly owes much to a manuscript tradition which includes reference to the sixteenth-century Ottoman invasion of Europe. However, the Scottish versions begin with the conception of a semi-divine hero in an enchanted dwelling or 'brugh', and this colours the whole tale since the hero has an inbuilt divine or fairy helper and, therefore does not need to depend on the standard heroic virtues! Even Conall Gulban's sword has a habit of winning battles without his assistance. Using such motifs, the storytellers reasserted their native traditions and absorbed other influences in a way that would continue to please their home audience with a diet of Loves, Elopements, Battles, Conceptions, Births, Voyages and Adventures, even if the old categories had become thoroughly intermingled within single tales and no longer individually acknowledged.

In some of the Hero Tales, the Romance elements are subordinate to a tighter structure of narrative and imagery. 'The Young King of Easaidh Ruadh' was recorded in 1859 from James Wilson, a blind fiddler in Islay, who had learnt it from an old man called Angus MacQueen some forty years earlier.[14] This story begins like 'Iain Og' with a gaming encounter between the hero and a 'brown, curly, long-haired' Gruagach. The stakes are played three times against the young king's newly wed wife who was herself won on the first wager. The hero is put under a spell but his wife now takes charge and sends him off to get the sword of light with which, under her instruction, he kills the Gruagach. But then he returns home to find his wife has been abducted by a giant. Now the hero shows love and determination and sets out to recover his wife and, in this quest, he is assisted by a dog, a hawk and an otter. The giant's soul turns out to be in an egg in the belly of a duck in the stomach of a sheep, so it proves decisive that the dog can catch the sheep, the hawk can pinion the duck, which takes flight when the sheep is cut open, and the otter can recover the egg when it rolls from the duck's belly into the depth of the ocean. When the woman, now described as Easaidh Ruadh's queen, breaks the egg the giant falls dead and the young couple can return home to resume 'raising music and laying down woe'.

This kind of story is sometimes called a Wonder Tale and the motifs involved are repeated in what are labelled International Tales because similar patterns and images are found across cultures.[15] This is not a case of literary influence because these tales predate literature, nor primarily of migration since they arise in too many different places from parallel life experiences. Though Hero Romances may contain similar motifs, they are subordinate in that context to a different overall tone and purpose. The Wonder Tales seem at once both more strange and more down to earth. They exhibit a natural magic, including a power of shape-changing or metamorphosis, which overcomes hostile supernatural powers and may reinforce, in an entertaining way, a wisdom about life which is lacking in the more artfully rollicking Romances. Wonder Tales are also amenable to the kind of sensitive contemporary retelling or reworking which the more extended Hero Tales elude.

Nineteenth-century Highland storytellers told Fenian stories, Hero Tales and Romances and Wonder Tales, but these categories do not exhaust the reservoir of Gaelic oral tradition. For, alongside these imaginative genres, there exists a huge body of Clan stories and traditions relating to the chiefs of the kin-based groupings which, after the decline of the Lordship of the Isles, were the principal social and military movers of Highland society. As J. F. Campbell's tale-collecting endeavours bore fruit, the Duke of Argyll employed John Dewar, one of Campbell's collectors, to gather traditional Gaelic material, resulting in seven manu-script volumes of meticulously scribed text, based on oral recording. These volumes, which were compiled by J. F. Campbell, comprised traditions about clan chiefs, detailed local history about the Jacobite Risings and their aftermath, and a record of the early dispossessions and dispersals of native Gaelic populations at home and abroad.[16]

Much of this material has a strong historical base and, without it, our understanding of the Highlands would be much the poorer. Nonetheless, the subject matter of these traditions is uncannily close to the Elopements, Battles, Cattle Raids and Tragic Deaths of older tradition. Clan chiefs replace the mythological heroes but continue to embody the collective aspirations of their tribes or clans, just as the eulogies and laments of classical Gaelic poetry focus on the fates and fortunes of these same chiefs. Supernatural motifs also play an important part in clan legends, while the often bloody events of clan tradition add an important strand to *Dindseanchas* – the lore and legend of place. Clan legends are geographically specific and provide every part of the Highlands and Islands with a local identity and tradition.

The folk tale is the principal transmitter of the clan histories, though there is also a dramatic realism which mirrors the harsh tones of Lowland chroniclers such as Lindsay of Pitscottie and is quite foreign to the fantastic Hero Tales and Romances. The issues driving clan legends are immediate ones concerning possession of land, leadership and even life itself. If the Wonder Tales later recited in the croft-houses of well-known storytellers were an indication of the psychological and spiritual health of Gaelic communities, then the Clan Tales were about their survival. The storytelling tradition reveals clan chiefs as the direct successors of the earlier culture's heroes, which goes some way to explaining why, when the chiefs or fathers of their people turned into commercial landlords, the fabric of Gaelic society collapsed.

Among the clan tales are many origin legends. Clan MacCodrum of the Uists, for example, is supposed to derive from a union between the clan's progenitor and a seal woman. As in most Selkie stories, the woman finds the skin which her husband has concealed and she returns to her seal form and the sea, leaving her human offspring to become ancestors of the clan. Although folk tradition has shaped this story according to selkie convention, there is clear suggestion of a totemic clan animal which reflects the life sources of the tribe or sept. Members of Clan MacCodrum, it was believed, were humans by day and seals by night.

Some early legends are closer to Romance than myth. One historical figure in the early annals of Clan Campbell is the Black Knight of Loch Awe, Sir Colin Campbell.[17] This knight goes on Crusade, leaving his bride with one half of a golden ring and a promise that he will return in seven years. The faithful lady guards the clan but she is wooed by neighbouring landowners, notably the Chief of MacCorquodale. Seven years elapse without news of the Black Knight until MacCorquodale arranges for a false palmer to bring word of Sir Colin's death. Still the faithful lady prevaricates, intimating that she must build a castle at the head of Loch Awe before she can marry. When the castle is complete this Penelope of Argyll can hold out no longer and her marriage to MacCorquodale is announced. But, on the eve of the wedding, a beggar arrives at the door. When admitted, he turns out, on production of the other half of the golden ring, to be Sir Colin himself. MacCorquodale is put to flight and the power of the Campbells takes root in the newly built stronghold of Kilchurn. Homer's *Odyssey* is an obvious literary influence here but Highland listeners would be more alert to the explanation of how the Campbells came to dominate the MacCorquodales and gain ownership of Glen Orchy.

The land and its control are a key concern of the Clan stories, as is demonstrated by another well-known legend about the disputes between the Camerons of Lochiel and the Men of Atholl.[18] Dissensions centre on where exactly their boundaries are set in the doubtful ground of Rannoch, where Inverness-shire, Argyll and Perthshire meet. The two sides agree to a parley at a small loch in the heart of the disputed territory. Each chief is to attend accompanied only by his piper. En route, however, Cameron of Lochiel is warned by a spey wife, or witch, that he must not go without armed guard – 'Where are your men, Lochiel?' she says, 'Where are your men?' So Lochiel positions his men behind a ridge. Atholl arrives with his piper but no agreement is reached and tempers rise till Atholl throws off his coat and his armed clansmen appear from behind another ridge. 'Who are these men?' accuses Lochiel. 'Oh,' says Atholl, 'they are Atholl sheep come to graze on Lochiel's pastures.' At this, Lochiel throws off his cloak and his armed retainers appear to their chief's rejoinder, 'These are Lochiel's dogs, hungry to attack Atholl's sheep'. According to the Dewar manuscripts, a battle was then fought in which Atholl was captured and forced to resign his territorial claim. This account may reflect Cameron tradition, for, according to a more local version, the chiefs came to terms and Atholl cast his sword into the loch as a pledge of their peace, so giving it its name, Loch of the Swords. When, in the nineteenth century, a schoolboy dragged up the sword it was thrown back so that the peace should not be broken.[19]

Peacemaking, however, is not the prevailing catalyst of the clan stories since pride and honour are as strongly motivating forces as the desire for land and power. One vivid example is the stormy relationship between the Colquhouns of Luss and the MacFarlanes of Tarbert and Arrochar, also traced in the Dewar manuscripts.[20] When MacFarlane discovers that his lady is spending a lot of time near Luss, apparently studying local weaving techniques, he immediately transforms suspicion into armed intrusion. Colquhoun has to run for his life to his castle in Glen Fruin but, in a classic Highland tactic, is smoked out by fire and slain. Then the MacFarlanes cut off Sir Humphrey Colquhoun's head and genitals, serving up the latter to Lady MacFarlane in a wooden dish with the words 'That is your share'. Needless to say divorce follows and Colquhoun/MacFarlane relations are strained for some time to come.

Theft, guile, burning and revenge are the stuff of clan tales but not exclusively. There are also stories of loyalty and honour. Once, when a MacGregor of Glenstrae and a

Lamont of Cowal were out hunting in Glen Etive, a violent quarrel arose and Lamont killed the young MacGregor.[21] Fleeing for his life, Lamont found himself in the early hours in Glenstrae and, seeing lights, sought refuge from his pursuers. There, according to Highland custom, he was granted protection by the Chief of Glenstrae, whose son he had murdered. When this became known, old MacGregor refused to give up the fugitive and conveyed him under safe keeping to Loch Fyne. Years later, the MacGregors were driven from Glenstrae by Clan Campbell and their aged chief became an outlaw in his turn. Despite the power of the Campbells, this fugitive was given refuge in Castle Toward, the stronghold of the Lamonts.

Some Clan Tales take the form of encounters with supernatural creatures, such as waterhorses, fairies and witches or sorceresses, so absorbing the chiefs into folklore. Donald Chief of Clan Mackay, for example, goes to the Witch of Reay to see if he can get a bridge built over the Kyle of Tongue.[22] She refers him on to the Witch of Tarbat who is in contact with bridge-building fairies. This witch commits a special box to Mackay's messenger, strictly warning him not to open the lid. Of course, he does and is immediately belaboured by fairies seeking work. Neither the messenger nor Chief Donald could keep these hyperactive fairies in work, till the exasperated Mackay ordered them to build a chain of sand across the Kyle. The fairies then disappeared but the rope of sand can still be seen as the tide recedes.

This light-hearted folk tale is very different from the historical traditions surrounding the Jacobite Risings and their consequences across the Highlands after Culloden. The Dewar manuscripts contain an extended, almost novelistic, account of the Appin Stewarts and their persecution following the Forty-five. At the core of this narrative is the Appin Murder in which Colin Campbell of Glenure, the oppressive factor of the confiscated Appin estates, was ambushed and shot. Although James Stewart, brother of the exiled clan chief, was hanged for the murder, it was probably the responsibility of a group of Stewart tacksmen acting in concert. For the Jacobite Highlands, the Appin

Murder became symbolic of Hanoverian oppression (with Campbell collusion) and of the capacity of Gaelic society still to resist. Robert Louis Stevenson derives part of his plot for the novel *Kidnapped* from this tale, since Alan Breck Stewart is a historical figure who claimed responsibility for the murder from overseas in order to protect his clansmen. The Appin Murder can be compared to the story of the Seven Men of Glen Moriston who never surrendered after the Forty-five but fought a guerrilla war from the remotest corners of their clan territory.

Local traditions in the Highlands continued to deploy oral narrative to social and cultural purpose, despite the breakdown of clan cohesion and the tendency of nine-teenth-century chiefs to treat their land as a personal eco-nomic asset rather than a collective inheritance. In illustration of this, the twentieth-century collector, Calum MacLean, cites the story of 'The Gaick Catastrophe' in which Captain James MacPherson of Ballachroan and his hunting party lost their lives in 1800.[23] Official accounts ascribe this tragedy to a fierce storm and avalanche which swept away their stone-built bothy in the forest of Gaick. Oral tradition, however, calls MacPherson the Black Officer, due not to his dark colouring but to his ruthless tactics as a recruiting officer for the Napoleonic wars. MacPherson's favourite ruse was to lure local men into an inn and plant the King's shilling in their pockets. The Black Officer was clearly in league with the Dark One and, shortly before Christmas 1800, the Devil came for his own. Sheltering in the Gaick bothy, the hunting party heard a knock at the door. 'Tonight is the night', said the messenger at the door and, when the corpses were found the following day, they were scattered far and wide, twisted and bruised, and wearing an expression of terror. Only by appeal to the name of the Devil could the Captain's body be carried home – 'a faithful servant', in Calum MacLean's words, 'of two principalities, the British Empire and the Powers of Darkness'!

MacLean's reflections on the Gaick catastrophe give rise to this well-known dictum: there are two histories of every land and people, the written history that tells what is considered politic to tell and the unwritten history that tells everything.[24] This perspective is certainly appropriate to the story of the Highlands and Islands of Scotland since 1745. Clearance, emigration, depopulation and militarisation shaped an oppressive written history of Gaelic Scotland. Until the late twentieth century, these externally imposed policies were accompanied by a denial of Gaelic culture and language in the official education system. Oral tradition, however, continued under severe social and economic pressure to be a lifeline to the Gaelic past and a resource for the future. At the start of the twenty-first century, under a newly devolved Scottish Parliament, the question remains as to whether enough of Gaelic society's cultural integrity remains to enable a renaissance for the benefit of Gaeldom and Scotland as a whole. If this is to be achieved, then Scots of whatever origin will have to come to terms with what the Highlands and Islands have to say about their own past.

Stories of clearances, emigrations and world war contrast strangely with the image of the Highlands so successfully promoted by James Macpherson's *Poems of Ossian* in the eighteenth century and by the Scottish Tourist Board in the twentieth. Writing in the aftermath of the Forty-five, Macpherson's desire was to restore a pride in Highland culture by appealing to the Romantic desire for closeness to wild nature.[25] Turning to the perfectly genuine traditions of Cuchulain and Fionn, he constructed a literary edifice based on the presumption that the Fenian tales and ballads were fragments of a lost Caledonian epic in the style of Homer's *Iliad.* This, he hoped, would provide Scotland with its own national epic to rival Italy's *Aeneid* and England's *Paradise Lost.* Such an epic would enable the bitterly divided Highlands and Lowlands to unite around a patriotic cultural project. By foregrounding the Highland's martial prowess, the project would also serve the cause of Empire. Moreover, the pristine virtues of the ancient Caledonian race would catch the mood and respond to the yearning of an increasingly urbanised Europe for a simpler and more noble civilisation.

Macpherson's achievement in creating a plangent lyric

and narrative otherworld has often been underrated. Starting from the Fenian ballads, he retains something of the natural imagery and nostalgic tone of his originals. But his real innovation is to combine the classical inheritance he had imbibed at Aberdeen University with the new Romantic yearning for pathos, tenderness and sublimity. However, his narrative structure is clearly based on Homer rather than any Gaelic sources. In arguing for the virtues of *Ossian*, Hugh Blair, Professor of Rhetoric at Edinburgh University and *Ossian*'s principal advocate, unconsciously reveals the source of Macpherson's narrative form in his first epic 'translation', *Fingal*:

> The story which is the foundation of the *Iliad* is in itself as simple as that of Fingal. A quarrel arises between Achilles and Agamemnon concerning a female slave; on which Achilles, apprehending himself to be injured, withdraws his assistance from the rest of the Greeks. The Greeks fall into great distress, and beseech him to be reconciled to them. He refuses to fight for them in person, but sends his friend Patroclus; and upon his being slain, goes forth to avenge his death and kills Hector. The subject of Fingal is this: Swaran comes to invade Ireland: Cuchullin, the guardian of the young King, had applied for assistance to Fingal, who reigned in the opposite coast of Scotland. But before Fingal's arrival he is hurried by rash counsel to encounter Swaran. He is defeated; he retreats; and desponds. Fingal arrives in this conjuncture. The battle is for some time dubious; but in the end he conquers Swaran; and the remembrance of Swaran's being the brother of Agandecca, who had once saved his life, makes him dismiss him honourably.[26]

Macpherson's dependence on narrative models that are alien to his source material has impaired the capacity of his reworking of Gaelic tradition to contribute to the ongoing development of Scottish storytelling, as opposed to a more diffuse Romantic consciousness.

In the latter, however, it could be argued that James

Macpherson was only too successful. Through 'Ossian', Macpherson and then Sir Walter Scott, a Romantic image of the Highlands became indelibly stamped on the wider cultural imagination and the temptation ever since has been for Scots – including Highland Scots – to play to the stereotype rather than the reality. Tragically, this led to a neglect of the true riches of Gaelic tradition in favour of a bland twilit world of Celtic bards, whose mystic inspiration draws us ever westwards into the land of the ever fading. The purpose of Gaelic tradition, by contrast, is to highlight the land in which we live, to imaginatively deepen and extend every aspect of human experience and to tell a story which is more, not less, than the sum of what history, in its more limited sense, can convey.

It is revealing that this work of imagination was located at the functional centre of the key institutions of Gaelic society – the chief's household and the domestic hearth. When the traditional hierarchies of Scottish Gaelic society went into decline, along with the older aristocratic order in the eighteenth century, the hearth took on a wider role, sustaining, not only the family culture, but the public traditions of the community. This is why the written and the oral, the aristocratic and the folk, are so richly inter-mingled in Scottish Gaelic storytelling. The twentieth-century scholar, Donald Archie MacDonald, describes a tradition which lingered in Hebridean communities until World War II:

> Tales seem to have been told on almost any occasion when people met together socially or for communal work. It could be a wake or a wedding, a funeral or a fair, or any number of other occasions, but by far the most important focus, cer-tainly during the nineteenth century and well into the twentieth, was the céilidh house. Every township had at least one such house which was distinguished as a popular meet-ing-place and in these people gathered together to tell and listen to stories, to sing songs, to exchange local news and gossip, even occasionally to play cards or to dance. The normal evening work of the household such as spinning or

carding or the twisting of the heather-rope would often continue during much of the time, but when serious story-telling started close attention and strict silence were usually expected, apart from relevant exclamations aroused by some incident or, of course, critical or appreciative comment when a tale or a session was finished. There was a traditional formula, not always adhered to, that the first tale should be told by the man of the house and tales could then be told till dawn by the guests. In practice, however, it seems to have been unusual in recent times for such sessions to go on much after midnight. Such evenings of communal enter-tainment are well within the memory of people still living.[27]

Notes

1. See Rees, Alwyn and Rees, Brinley (1961), *Celtic Heritage: Ancient Tradition in Ireland and Wales*, London: Themes and Hudson, pp. 207–12.
2. See Aarne, Antii and Thompson, Stith (1964), *The Types of the Folktale*, Helsinki: FF Communications, passim for an exhaus-tive catalogue of tale types and motifs such as 'The King's Tasks', 'The Girl as Helper in the Hero's Flight', 'The Entrapped Suitors', 'The Rich and the Poor Peasant' and so on.
3. For the best modern translation from the twelfth-century Irish manuscripts see *The Tain*, translated by Kinsella, Thomas (1969), Oxford: Oxford University Press.
4. For a detailed account of the surviving Irish and Scottish manuscript traditions see Bruford, Alan (1969), *Gaelic Folk Tales and Medieval Romances*, Dublin: Folklore of Ireland Society, pp. 250–67.
5. Ibid.
6. See Dillon, Myles (1994), *Early Irish Literature*, Dublin: Four Courts Press, pp. 32–50.
7. Ibid. pp. 37–8.
8. See, for example, 'The Lay of Diarmaid' (No. LXI) in Camp-bell, J. F. (1890–3), *Popular Tales of the West Highlands*, Vol. III, 2nd Ed., Paisley: Alexander Gardner. For specific collections of Scottish Fenian material see Campbell, Lord Archibald, *Waifs and Strays of Celtic Tradition*, Vol. 4; Campbell, John Gregson (1891), *The Fians*, London: David Nutt; and Camp-

bell, J. F. (1972), *Leabhar na Feinne*, Vol. I only, Dublin: Irish Universities Press.

9. See MacLellan, Angus (1961), *Stories from South Uist* trans. Campbell, J. L., London: Routledge and Kegan Paul, p. 3.

10. See MacDonald D. A. 'Gaelic Storytelling, Traditional', in Daiches, David (ed.), *The New Companion to Scottish Culture* pp. 121–3 for a succinct account of the historical interlinking of the aristocratic and folk traditions.

11. Campbell, J. F. (1940), *More West Highland Tales* transcribed and translated by Mackay, John A., Vol. I ed. Watson, W. J., MacLeod, D., and Rose, H. J., Edinburgh: Oliver and Boyd:, pp. 228–77.

12. Ibid. p. 237.

13. See Bruford, Alan and MacDonald, Donald A. (ed.) (1994), *Scottish Traditional Tales,* Edinburgh: Polygon, pp. 139–52.

14. See *Popular Tales of the West Highlands*, Vol. I, No. 1, pp. 1–24.

15. See *Scottish Traditional Tales*, pp. 11–18 for a succinct account of these broad classifications of stories by early folktale scholars.

16. See *The Dewar Manuscripts* collected by Dewar, John, trans. MacLean, Hector, Vol. I, *Scottish West Highland Folk Tales* ed. Mackechnie, John (1964), Glasgow: William MacLellan.

17. Sir Colin Campbell of Glenorchy, the first Campbell laird of that territory who died in 1480, is described in the earliest records as 'a knight of Rhodes' but little is known historically about his crusading involvements. However, romance clusters around him in both written and oral sources. In the Inventory of Taymouth Castle, there is the following intriguing entry: 'ane stone of the quantitye of half a hen's eg set in silver, being flat at the ane end and round at the uther end lyke a peir, whilk Sir Colin Campbell first laird of Glenurchy wore when he fought in battell at the Rhodes agaynst the Turks, he being one of the knychts of the Rhodes'. This surviving brooch or amulet was later held to have protective powers. See *The Black Book of Taymouth*, Edinburgh: Marquis of Breadalbane (1855), pp. ii–iii and pp. 10–14.

18. See *The Dewar Manuscripts* Vol. I, pp. 89–91.

19. See MacGregor, Alasdair Alpin (1937), *The Peat-Fire Flame: Folk-Tales and Traditions of the Highlands and Islands*, Edinburgh: Ettrick Press, pp. 275–7.

20. See *The Dewar Manuscripts* Vol. I, pp. 115–19.

21. See *The Peat-Fire Flame: Folk-Tales and Traditions of the Highlands and Islands*, pp. 243–6.
22. See Temperley, Alan (1977), *Tales of the North Coast*, London: Research Publishing, pp. 110–14.
23. See MacLean, Calum (1994), *The Highlands*, 3rd Ed. Edinburgh: Mainstream, pp. 158–60. [Originally published London: Batsford, 1959.]
24. Ibid. p. 158.
25. For an excellent critical edition of these much mis-represented literary works, see *The Poems of Ossian and Related Works*, ed. Howard Gaskill (1996), with an introduction by Fiona Stafford, Edinburgh: Edinburgh University Press.
26. Ibid., p. 361. Note Blair's summary of his argument: 'Aristotle studied nature in Homer. Homer and Ossian both wrote from nature. No wonder that among all the three, there should be such agreement and conformity.' Ibid. p. 358.
27. MacDonald, D. A., 'Gaelic Storytelling, Traditional' in Daiches, David (ed.), *The New Companion to Scottish Culture*, p. 122.

Lowland Traditions

◆

The Gaelic traditions of storytelling which have been described in the previous chapter were also accessible to the royal court in its peregrinations about Scotland. Bards and harpers (sometimes combined in the one person), Romance reciters and folk tale tellers would be made welcome at a Gaelic-speaking court. However, from the twelfth century, other European traditions of storytelling and Romance were becoming influential in Scotland. David I, son of Malcolm Canmore and the Saxon Queen Margaret, may have favoured the chansons and gestes of the continental chivalric Romances as an integral aspect of a cultural, political and religious project to bring Scotland into the European mainstream. The story in which David sets out hunting on Holy Cross Day, against his confessor's advice, and, encountering a ferocious stag at bay, grasps its antlers only to be left holding a cross, is a piece of conscious saintly romancing which provides the foundation legend for Holyrood Abbey. David's grandson, William the Lion, counted among his closest advisers the Anglo-Norman cleric, Bishop William Malveisin, who is believed to be the author of the literary *Romance Fergus of Galloway*.[1]

To some extent these continental influences capitalised on neglected aspects of native tradition. Encouraged by the popularity of the 'Matter of Britain' in European Romance, which was also reflected in the publication of Geoffrey of Monmouth's *History* in 1137, the Scottish kings emphasised their own Arthurian connections, embodied in place names such as Arthur's Seat and Edinburgh Castle's traditional epithet, 'Castle of the Maidens'. Admittedly, the role of Scotland in most of the chivalric Romances is that of a conventionally fantastic northern land, but some key stories, such as 'Tristan and Iseult' are strongly Celtic in ethos and tone.[2] There is also evidence of the spread of Arthurian tradition in Gaelic storytelling, not least in Argyll, and one Arthurian ballad 'Am Bron Binn' or 'The Sweet Sorrow' survived in oral memory until the twentieth century.[3]

The medieval picture is one of mixed influences, with Gaelic traditions, French Romances and Latin models, such as Saints' Legends, all employed by the Scottish court and aristocracy. Professional artists representing these different strands would be employed as performers operating both from oral memory and manuscripts. Court and aristocratic halls were also the focuses of historical traditions and legends, regarding the deeds of distinguished ancestors and the rise and fall of landowning warrior dynasties; the feudal Scots nobility looked to their heralds to act as historians and poets, in the same way as Gaelic chiefs looked to their bards and genealogists.

But, during the twelfth and thirteenth centuries, there was also a major linguistic development as Middle English, in a distinctively Scots form, gained ascendancy over the Celtic languages (Gaelic and Brythonic/Welsh) in southern and eastern Scotland, so paving the way for the emergence of Scots as the primary speech of what can now be described as the Lowlands. The speed with which Middle English and its Scots cousin displace French as the local vehicle for literary Romance indicates the relative weakness of Anglo-Norman influence in comparison to native traditions about which we know very little. However, a distinctively Lowland Scots version of storytelling now begins to emerge into the light of later generations.

Our knowledge of this early period is very incomplete but John of Fordun quotes from a verse narrative about Malcolm Canmore, which may also be the source for Walter Bower and Andrew of Wyntoun's account of Macbeth.[4] This same narrative, as embroidered by Hector Boece, was to provide Shakespeare with his Scottish plot. The Middle English Romance of Sir Orfeo seems to have emerged in Scotland at this time and exhibits strong Celtic influence.[5] Orfeo wanders, inconsolable, for years until he sees his lost love among a fairy band and pursues her into the otherworld, from where she is successfully recovered to the land of the living. This version of the Orpheus myth survived in an oral ballad until the nineteenth and twentieth centuries, when it was recorded in Shetland.[6] It is also inconceivable that legends, folk tales and ballads concerning the deeds of William Wallace and Robert the Bruce were not in early and popular circulation. Andrew of Wyntoun refers to 'grete gestes' of Wallace's 'dedes and manheid' which were subsumed and, to a large extent, displaced by the huge success of Barbour's *Bruce* and Blind Hary's *Wallace* to be discussed shortly.

Another tantalising insight into this earliest period of Lowland Scots storytelling is the chivalric Romance of Sir Tristrem which is ascribed to Thomas the Rhymer, whom we met earlier in a more mythical disguise in the clutches of the Fairy Queen. In its surviving form, Sir Tristrem is linguistically more Middle English than Scots but Thomas is identified as the author by a contemporary, Robert Mannyng de Brunne, who complains that the metrical intricacies of the poem were mangled when it was not recited as composed by the author.[7]

A further Romance of Thomas the Rhymer, entitled *Thomas of Erceldoune*, survives in a fragmentary manuscript form at Lincoln Cathedral. In this Romance, the hero is taking his ease on Huntly Bank when he is approached by none other than the Fairy Queen:

> In a lade as I was lent,
> In the gryking of the day
> Ay alone as I went,
> In Huntle bankys me for to play;
> I saw the throstyl, and the jay,
> Ye mawes movyde of her song,
> Ye wodwale sange notes gay,
> That al the wod about range.
> In that longyng as I lay,
> Undir nethe a dern tre,

> I was war of a lady gay,
> Come ryding ouyr a fair le:
> Zogh I suld sitt to domysday,
> With my tong to wrabbe and wry,
> Certenly all hyr array,
> It beth neuer discryuyd for me.[8]

Clearly this is a mirror image for the ballad of 'Thomas the Rhymer':

> True Thomas lay on Huntlie bank
> A ferlie he spied wi his ee:
> And there he saw a ladye bright,
> Come riding down by the Eildon Tree.[9]

In the Romance, the Fairy Queen gives the hero many strange prophecies of the kind later ascribed to 'Thomas the Rhymer'.

For Sir Walter Scott, who collected Thomas the Rhymer in his *Minstrelsy of the Scottish Border (1802–3)*, this is a clear example of the way in which an aristocratic Romance passes into folk tradition and is thereby simplified metrically in a way that can be easily remembered and sung. Scott paraphrases, in his support, the contemporary complaint of de Brunne and is inclined to suggest that the ballad represents a lower art form, sung 'in vulgar dialect' to 'an inferior audience'. However, confronted with the sheer quality of the ballad, 'Thomas the Rhymer', Scott trims his argument.

> We are left to conjecture whether the originals of such ballads have been gradually contracted into their modern shape by the impatience of later audiences, combined with the lack of memory displayed by more modern reciters, or whether in particular cases some ballad-maker may have actually set himself to retrench the old details of the minstrels, and regularly and systematically to modernise and, if the phrase be permitted, to balladise a metrical romance'.[10]

The art which produced stanzas like the following is hardly vulgar or inferior or less original or necessarily younger than that of the metrical Romance:

> Her shirt was o the grass green silk
> Her mantle o the velvet fyne;
> At ilka tett of her horse's mane
> Hung fifty siller bells and nine.[11]

As we have already established, the myth on to which Thomas the Rhymer is grafted is older than either the Romance or the ballad and a common property of Lowland and Highland tradition.

What Scott does not consider is that the oral traditions underlying the Thomas Romances and the ballad may reach back into the Brythonic culture of the early Celtic kingdom of southern Scotland – what is sometimes described as the age of Arthur. The emergence of Middle Scots and its vigorous literature is much more comprehensible if an underlying continuity is presumed from the landscape and language of the majority of the settled population.[12]

Thomas of Erceldoune, a real thirteenth-century Borderer who features in both Scots and Gaelic tradition as Thomas the Rhymer, becomes from this perspective the key poetic, or, more properly, bardic figure, reaffirming connection with the older Brythonic Celtic culture at a time when fears about the succession and the tragic death of Alexander III threatened to end two centuries of peace and prosperity. This also explains the later popularity of the Rhymer's prophecies in Highland Gaelic tradition, since they would form part of a common oral inheritance.

The Brythonic kingdom of Gododdin in the east ended with the defeat by the Anglo-Saxons at Catterick in 600. This is lamented in elegaic detail by the Gododdin bard, Aneirin, who provides in this poem the earliest datable reference to Arthur, already seen as a legendary hero.[13] However, the western kingdom of Strathclyde persisted under the saintly protection of Kentigern or Mungo until the ninth century and was not fully absorbed into the newly feudal kingdom of

Scotland until the twelfth. Hence the tradition that Arthur himself was still sleeping beneath the Eildon Hills where Thomas is granted his bardic fights, ready to return at a moment of crisis – a moment perhaps such as the one the Rhymer felt was looming. Since he was intellectually a Hanoverian Unionist and emotionally a Stewart loyalist, Sir Walter Scott was politically and psychologically unlikely to emphasise a cultural legacy older than either.

Scott's discussion does, however, raise a very interesting question about how the metrical Romances were performed. Did they have a musical accompaniment, were they sung or declaimed, and were they recited from memory or from manuscript? No certain answers are available to these questions but the waters have been considerably muddied by unrestrained use of the catch-all term 'minstrel', not least by Scott himself. It seems likely that some form of instrumental accompaniment backed up performance of the metrical Romances but in such a way as to provide a ground for vocal delivery of the words. A later fifteenth-century Romance, 'Greysteil' was sung by two fiddlers in 1497 for James IV and the tune survives in a lute version of 1627, perhaps echoing a clarsach setting.[14] The demands on timing and memory would make such a performance a considerable feat and it is not surprising that the metrically simpler and generally shorter ballad forms for unaccompanied singing were more popular. There is a parallel here with Gaelic tradition where the Fenian lays became a medium for unaccompanied singing, while the more metrically complex eulogies and laments of classical poetry remained the remit of bards and harpers.

Whether instrumental or vocal, the musical element retained high artistic and spiritual status in Gaelic tradition along with the words, whereas the Lowland Scots tradition has tended to emphasise transmission of the words with a loss of musical accompaniment. There is a hint of this emphasis within the Romance of *Thomas of Erceldoune* itself. In the Castle of Fairy, Thomas hears music aplenty:

> Harp and fedyl both he fande
> The getern and the sawtry,
> Lut and rybid ther gon gan,
> Thair was al maner of mynstralsy.[15]

However, Thomas's parting gift is the mixed blessing of prophecy and the choice of 'harp or carp' – to speak or play better than any other mortal. Thomas chooses speech 'for tongue is chief of mynstralsy' and even the Fairy Queen is concerned that Thomas should 'speak no ill of me'. Instrumental music, poetry, unaccompanied ballad singing and storytelling would all have their part to play in the growth of Scots Lowland tradition but minstrels as a professional class, distinct from musicians in general, remain elusive in the Scottish context.

The Scots language soon found its voice and subject matter through a period of extreme national trial and danger. There is a poignancy in the fact that one of the earliest recognisably Scots poems is a lament for the two centuries of relative stability between the reign of Malcolm Canmore and the death of Alexander III in 1286:

> Quhen Alexander our Kynge was dede
> That Scotland lede in lauche and le
> Away was sons of alle and brede
> Of wyne and wax, of gamyn and gle.
> Our golde was changit in to lede.
> Crist, born in virgynyte,
> Soccoure Scotlande, and remede,
> That stade is in perplexite.[16]

That the nation did not prove wanting in this ordeal is the inspiration of John Barbour's narrative poem, *The Bruce*, written in the 1370s under the patronage of Robert II. In writing *The Bruce*, Barbour used several sources – oral traditions, some form of earlier written collections about the lives of Robert the Bruce and Sir James Douglas, conventional medieval learning and the models of continental Romance. His subject is chivalry as exemplified by the Scottish leaders and he takes a high moral tone regarding the virtues of loyalty, courage, endurance and the value of freedom. However, Barbour is much closer to terra firma than the majority of Anglo-Norman Romances, since the conflict he depicts is genuinely a life and death struggle for the nation and its heroes and, moreover, one which had continued to engage the Scotland of his own time. The tone and subject matter of *The Bruce* is closer to the earlier epic Romance of the *Chanson de Roland* than the Arthurian gestes, and Barbour emphasises with his first words the distinctiveness of his purpose:

> Storys to rede ar delitabill
> Suppos that thai be nocht but fabill
> Than suld storys that suthfast wer
> And thai war said on gud maner
> Have doubill pleasance in heryng.[17]

The Bruce has many storytelling strengths. Firstly, there is the interweaving of two heroic biographies – that of Bruce and Douglas – from the earliest guerrilla struggles through to the latter's chivalric attempt to take the dead King's heart to the Holy Land. The topography of the poem is also accurate and vivid as conflict shifts from one part of Scotland to another, exposing the heroes to the vagaries of Scottish geography and local loyalties. The form of the narrative has the drive of the earlier metrical Romances but with greater flexibility and linguistic depth, making it a powerful vehicle for recitation and declamation in sections.

Finally, of course, *The Bruce* has, at its narrative heart, an extended set piece in the Battle of Bannockburn, the influence of which has resonated in Scottish popular consciousness. Within the battle sequence Bruce's address to the army is a dramatic high point:

> And when it comis to the ficht
> Ilk man set his heart and mycht
> To stynt our fayis mekill pride.
> On horse they sall arrrayit ride

And come on you in weill great hy:
Meet them with speris hardily,
And wreak on them the mekill ill
That they and theiris has done us till,
And are in will yet for to do,
Gif they have mycht till come there-to.
And, certis, me think weill that we
For-out abasing oucht till be,
Worthy and of great vassalage,
For we have three great avantage:
The first is that we have the richt;
And for the richt ilk man suld ficht.
The tothir is, they are comin here
For lypning in their great power,
To seek us in our awne land,
And has broucht here, rycht till our hand,
Riches into so great plenty
That the poorest of you sall be
Baith rich and mychty therewithal
Gif that we win, as weill may fall.
The thrid is, that we for our lyvis
And for our children and our wivis,
And for the fredome of our land,
Are strenyeit in battail for to stand;
And they for their mycht anerly,
And for they leit of us lichtly,
And for they wald destroy us all,
Mais them to ficht; bot yet may fall
That they sall rue their bargaining.[18]

Barbour is not inventing here but incorporates a previously existing source to great effect, echoing Calgacus's address to the Caledonians before the Battle of Mons Graupius (as devised by the Roman historian Tacitus) and anticipating Robert Burns's song, 'Scots Wha Hae'. It is a remarkable achievement that Barbour begins literature in Scots with a defining national narrative, strengthening the presumption that he is building on a tradition of oral poetry – much of which has been lost. *The Bruce* is more epic than Romance and its master narrative of triumph against great adversity was taken up by historians, poets and popular tradition alike.

The Bruce has a successor and companion piece in *The Wallace*, which was written a century later as an impassioned reminder of the patriotic virtues and in opposition to the pro-English policies of the Scottish court.[19] *The Wallace* is a heroic biography emphasising the subject's role as a popular champion and friend of the people. In many ways *The Wallace* is an even stronger piece of storytelling than *The Bruce*. The narrative is visually evocative with an almost physical realism. Moreover, it enters more deeply into the trial and tragedy of its hero than *The Bruce*, culminating in an extended account of martyrdom. *The Wallace* is also a highly crafted literary work drawing on history, poetry and philosophy, as well as the continental Romances and native traditions. The practical knowledge of war demonstrated by the author has led to the suggestion that he served as a soldier.[20]

The author of *The Wallace* is known as Blind Hary or Henry the Minstrel, though scholars have argued that he was neither a roving entertainer nor, at the time of writing, blind. The source of these presumptions is John Mair or Major who, in his 1518 *History of Britain,* states explicitly that Hary was blind from birth, that he gathered the popular tales about Wallace in skilled vernacular verse and that he earned 'the food and clothing that he so well deserved by storytelling in noble houses'. So the learned philosopher puts the 'popular' historian in his place.

Between 1490 and 1492, Blind Hary appears five times in the royal accounts as the recipient of payments from James IV, four of these occasions being near Easter or on New Year's Day.[21] These bounties appear amongst other payments to entertainers, supporting the presumption that Hary was present at Linlithgow Palace on these occasions as an honoured poet, either to recite part of his work or to hear such a recitation. This does not necessarily turn Hary into a wandering minstrel and, in fact, the available evidence seems to limit his court visits to Linlithgow. But it does give a fascinating glimpse into the diversity of entertainment at the court. Alongside Hary the Romance poet, trumpeters are rewarded as well as harpers, two of whom are specifically described as Gaelic or 'Ersche' clarsairs. Then Sir Thomas Galbraith, Jock Goldsmith and Crawford received their bounty 'for the singyn of a ballat to the King in the morning'. Fiddlers and singers in general also receive payments sometimes under the collective term 'menstralys'. The storytellers mentioned are not classified as minstrels and have other employments. One is a courier – 'Wallas that tauld geistis' – and another the royal fowler – 'Widderspune that tauld tales to the King'. Although the organisational structure appears less formal than in Gaelic tradition, the principle is the same: whatever the crossovers of shared subject matter or source material, each mode of narrative delivery requires different skills and has its own practitioners. A later Act of James VI against all manner of wandering entertainers, such as 'ydill beggaris, sornaris, fulis, bairds' as well as those using 'subtilee crafty and unlawful playis such as iuglerie', specifically excludes those entertainers attached to aristocratic houses or burgh councils. They are classified as 'menstralis (that is, musicians) sangstaris and taill tellaris'.[22]

Through the reign of James I and his successors, narrative art in Lowland Scotland continued to develop in three interweaving strands. Firstly, there was written literature embracing history, poetry, philosophy and later drama. Secondly, there was folk tale and, thirdly, sung ballads, which existed for some time alongside the metrical Romances but then superseded them. The written literature, spearheaded by the Scottish Makars, or poets, beginning with James I himself, included lyric and dramatic poetry as well as narrative, some of it designed for performance in a courtly setting.[23] The storytelling interest was central to the art of Robert Henryson who emulated Chaucer by producing a distinctive version of the Troilus and Cressida tale in his *Testament of Cresseid*, as well as an Orpheus and Eurydice poem and his humorous reworking of Aesop's Fables in a Northern European setting. The ease with which Henryson blends the classical and the vernacular sets a pattern for succeeding centuries. Gavin Douglas also measured the Scots vernacular against the epic tradition of the Latin *Aeneid* and did not find it wanting in his fine translation (the first into a European vernacular language), while Sir David Lyndsay rewrote the Romance Tale of chivalry in his realistic love story, *The Historie of Squyer Meldrum*.

Lyndsay's work capitalises on sixteenth-century awareness of the Romance conventions but the work of the Scots Makars as a whole points forward to a period when literature would be savoured by the solitary reader rather than recited or declaimed. The scholarly Henryson provides the prototype when, on a bleak February evening as 'schouris of haill cam fra the north discent/Thart scantlie fra the cauld I micht defend', he describes himself sitting down to read Chaucer's poem and then to write his own superb sequel:

> I mend the fyre and beikit me about,
> Then tuik ane drink my spreitis to comfort,
> And armit me weill fra the cauld thairout:
> To cut the winter nicht and mak it short,
> I tuik ane quair [*book*] and left all uther sport,
> Written be worthie Chaucer glorious
> Of fair Cresseid, and worthie Troylus.[24]

Henryson's is a subtle precise narrative art that needs the reflective eye as well as the ear.

There is a cluster of late medieval and Renaissance Scottish narrative poems which clearly imitate the Romance genre conventions in order to undercut them. In the anonymous 'The Taill of Rauf Coilyear' the Emperor Charlemagne arrives in disguise at the door of a Scottish collier only to find that Rauf is as insistent on his own rights as any high-born courtier.[25] In another anonymous poem 'The Colkelbie Sow' there is a series of scenes including a mock tournament, which are a burlesque of the Romance conventions. In the Bannatyne Manuscript of 1568, which is the most important sixteenth-century collection of Scottish poetry, the fifth and final section is devoted to narrative 'fabillis', including Henryson, the more satirically comic William Dunbar and 'The Colkelbie Sow'. Sixteenth-century literary tastes did not, however, wholly abandon the Romance aspiration. The late fifteenth-century 'Golagros and Gawane', translated into Scots from an earlier French chanson, maintains the tradition, while Ariosto's Renaissance masterpiece, *Orlando Furioso*, was wittily abridged in Scots as *Roland Furious* by John Stewart of Baldynnis under the patronage of James VI. In the *Orlando*, Scotland still figures as a fantastic northern territory but Stewart sweeps everything along in a highly entertaining dramatic narrative.[26]

Humour and strong dramatic action are equally characteristics of Scots folk tales. Most surviving Lowland folk narratives were recorded in the nineteenth or twentieth centuries but the tradition is certainly as old as the origins of Scots as a popular language. Robert Wedderburn's sixteenth-century *Complaynt of Scotland* mentions several folk tales, including 'Red Etin' and 'The Wal at the World's End', presuming that they were well known. Significantly, the catalogue of stories supplied by the *Complaynt* as part of a virtuoso display of vernacular rhetoric makes no distinction between folk tales, Romances or classical legends; between tales of Arthur, Bruce, Wallace, Orpheus, Hercules, Robin Hood, 'the giants that eat quyk [living] men', the three-footed dog of Norway or Rauf Coilyear. Furthermore, 'sum was in prose and sum was in verse, sum were storeis and sum were flet [plain] taylis'.[27] Of course, this is a rhetorical catalogue but it does give a flavour of the eclectic gusto of Scots storytelling during this period with its rich range of sources oral and written, native, English and European. There is also a suggestion in the distinction between 'storeis' or extended narratives and 'flet taylis' or short folk tales of differing styles and ambitions in the storyteller's art.

Several poems collected in the Asloan, Maitland and Bannatyne Manuscripts are folk tales in verse. These include the 'Gyre-Carling' which Sir David Lyndsay tells us he related to James V when he was a boy. In this Rabelaisian morsel, the carlin laughs 'and lut fart North Berwick Law'.

Then there is the abusive 'How the first heilandman of God was Maid of Ane Horss Turd in Argylle, as Is Said' and the richly humorous 'Wyf of Auchtermuchty' in which a nagging farmer insists on swapping roles with his spouse for a day.[28] The gudewife proves a dab hand at ploughing but the gudeman loses five goslings to a kite; the calves break loose and suck the cows before they have been milked; the milk will not churn; and, in a clumsy attempt to stop a sow draining the churn, the hapless house-husband kills the two remaining goslings. Then the gudeman finds that in the meantime his bairns have soiled the bed and, when he attempts to wash the sheets, they are swept away as the burn is in spate. At that he gives in and begs his wife to take back her share of the work. The 'Wyf of Auchtermuchty' has all the characteristics of the classic Scots folk tale, except for the vital element of magic – unless, of course, in an earlier version, the gudewife triumphed because she had cast bad magic on the day's domestic proceedings!

Alongside vivid characterisation, clear dramatic structure and vigorous direct speech, the Lowland Scots folk tales share with the Gaelic world the natural supernaturalism of the Wonder Tales and the plot devices and motifs of the International folk tales or Marchen. 'The Red Etin of Ireland', for example, is a Scots version of 'Jack the Giant Killer'. The hero lad is a youngest son who sees his two older brothers take a 'hale cake' from their mother 'and her malison along wi't'. Off each goes to seek their fortune but all they meet with is a fearful warning:

> The Red Etin of Ireland
>   Ance lived in Bellygan,
> He stole King Malcolm's daughter,
>   The king of fair Scotland.
> He beats her, he binds her,
>   He lays her on a band;
> And every day he dings her
>   With a bright silver wand.
> Like Julian the Romand
>   He's one that fears no man.

> It's said there's ane predestinate
>   To be his mortal foe;
> But that man is yet unborn,
>   And lang may it be so.[29]

Pressing on, they come to the Etin's Castle and go in for shelter. Then the three-headed giant comes home:

> Snouk but and snouk ben
> I find the smell of an earthly man;[30]

Both boys in succession are asked three questions which they cannot answer and are turned to stone. The young hero now sets out with a half cake and his mother's blessing. In a canny Scots touch, however, he has plugged the leaky jar in which he fetches water from the well for the baking, so his half cake is bigger than the brothers' whole ones. Then he shares his bannock with an old woman on the way and she gives him a magic wand which carries him through danger to the Etin's Castle, where he answers the three questions, cuts off the ogre's three heads and releases from captivity a lovely young woman who turns out to be the king's daughter.

Many of the Scots tales have doughty heroines reflecting a fireside tradition borne by women rather than men. Mally Whuppie is a formidable giant-slayer who turns every adversity on its head to win the king's youngest son. The Scots Cinderella, Rashiecoats, is a strong-minded lass who refuses the husband picked by her father – 'and her father wanted her to be married; but she didna like the man' – and sets out to seek her fortune.[31] In 'Whuppity Stoorie', the Scots Rumpelstiltskin, the gudewife, having been outwitted by a fairy, turns the tables:

> Aweel, ye maun ken that this goodwife was a jokus woman, and aye merry when her heart wasna unco sair owreladen. Sae she thinks to hae some sport wi' the fairy; and, at the appointit time she puts the bairn behint the knockin'-stane, and sits down on't hersel'. Syne she pu's her mutch ajee owre her left lug, crooks her mou on the tither side, as gin she war

greetin', and a filthy face she made, you may be sure. She hadna lang to wait, for up the brae mounts the green fairy, nowther lame nor lazy; and lang or she gat near the knockin'-stane she skirls out: 'Goodwife o Kittletumpit, ye weel ken what I come for – stand and deliver!' The wife pretends to greet sairer than before, and wrings her nieves, and fa's on her knees wi': 'Och, sweet madam mistress, spare my only bairn, and take the weary soo!'

'The deil take the soo for my share,' qu' the fairy; 'I come na here for swine's flesh. Dinna be contramawcious, hizzie, but gie me the gett instantly.'

'Ochone dear leddy mine,' quo' the greetin' goodwife; 'forbear my poor bairn and take mysel'!'

'The deil's in the daft jad,' quo' the fairy, looking like the faur end o' a fiddle; 'I'll wad she's clean dementit. Wha in a' the earthly warld, wi' half an ee in their head, wad ever meddle wi' the likes o' thee?'

I trow this set up the wife of Kittlerumpit's birse; for though she had twa bleert een, and a lang red neb forbye, she thought hersel' as bonny as the best o' them. Sae she bangs aff her knees, sets up her mutch-croon, and wi' her twa hands faulded afore her, she maks a curchie down to the grund and, 'In troth, fair madam,' quo' she, 'I might hae had the wit to ken that the likes o' me is na fit to tie the warst shoe-strings o' the heich and mighty princess, Whuppity Stoorie!'

Gin a fluff o' gunpowder had come oot o' the ground, it coudna hae gart the fairy loup heicher nor she did; syne doon she came again, dump on her shoe-heels, and whurlin' round, she ran down the brae, scraichin' for rage, like a houlet chased wi' the witches.[32]

In these Scots tales the international motifs are thoroughly indigenised and dramatised. Sometimes the supernatural is humorously treated but there are also tales of witches, warlocks and fairy changelings which carry an older charge of belief. In the 'Milk-White Doo,' which became a popular nursery tale, a stepmother feeds her husband with his daughter but a sister 'gathered aa the banes and put them in below a stone at the cheek o the door, where they grew and they grew/To a milk white doo'.[33]

'The Black Bull o Norroway' is a Wonder Tale in which the heroine rides a magic bull who fights with the devil. Lost and alone, she then has to undergo a series of trials to win her knight, an enchanted husband:

> Seven lang years I served for thee
> The glassy hill I clamb for thee
> The bluidy shirt I wrang for thee
> Will thou no wauken and turn to me?[34]

Many of the best versions of these tales were collected by Robert Chambers in the nineteenth century or by the School of Scottish Studies at Edinburgh University in the twentieth. Chambers' 'Whuppity Stoorie' is of particular interest since he sourced it from an Edinburgh literateur, Charles Kirkpatrick Sharpe, who claimed that he was recalling it word for word from the eighteenth-century telling of his Dumfriesshire nurse, Jenny from Hoddam. Therefore, his account begins, unusually for this period, with a definite context:

> I ken ye're fond o clashes aboot fairies, bairns; and a story anent a fairy and the goodwife o Kittlerumpit has joost come into my mind . . . The goodman o' Kittlerumpit was a vaguing sort o' a body; and he gaed to a fair ae day, and not only never came hame again but never mair was heard o'. Some said he listed, and ither some that the waerifu' press gang cleekit him up, though he was clothed wi' a wife and a wean forbye. Hech-How! That dulefu' press gang! They gaed about the kintra like roarin' lions, seekin' who they micht devoor. I mind weel, my auldest brither Sandy was a' but smoored in the meal ark hiding frae thae limmers. After they war gane we pu'd him oot frae amang the meal, pechin' and greetin' and as white as ony corp. Ma mither had to pike the meal oot o' his mooth wi' the shank o' a horn spoon.[35]

Nurse Jenny has blended into her narration, as a pre-story or anecdote, an eighteenth-century incident about press gangs told in the same vivid Scots and with the same sense of dramatic action. In this way, master storytellers wove past and present, natural and supernatural, history and legend into a unified narrative texture. The meal kist incident elaborates a possible reason for the gudeman's disappearance and skilfully anticipates the domestic resource that will be needed in the main tale. The reference to 'my auldest brither Sandy' artfully draws the listeners by degrees into the much less familiar territory of a 'green leddy' who claims to have suffered 'waur losses at the Shirra Muir' and administers cures with the suspiciously 'papist' spell *Pitter patter/ Haly water*. This naturalisation or contextualisation of the supernatural is more characteristic of Lowland Scots storytelling than of the Scottish Gaelic or Traveller traditions, where the storyteller seems to have felt little need to mediate the magical to his or her audience.

As in Gaelic storytelling, however, the Wonder Tales, Romances and Hero Tales were complemented in Lowland areas by a wealth of historical stories and legends of place which have continued in popular currency to the present day. Where Gaelic tales featured clan chiefs, Lowland Scots had their kings and the heads of great aristocratic dynasties – Gordon, Moray, Douglas, Kennedy – who competed for land, favour and honour. These stories carried Scottish audiences through the fifteenth- and sixteenth-century Stewart line and the Civil Wars of the seventeenth century to the Jacobite struggles of the eighteenth, building seamlessly on the work of the earlier chroniclers and historians. Democratisation, though, sets in earlier in Lowland history than in Highland, as kings and lords are supplemented and later supplanted in Scots stories by millers, gudemen, wabsters, gudewifes, packmen, soldiers, serving lassies and beggars. This, of course, does not apply to the timeless heroes and heroines of Wonder Tales who evade social restrictions.

Scots storytellers exploited a remarkable raw material in the lives and deaths of the Stewart kings, which sometimes seem larger than folklore. James I, the courtly poet, was brutally murdered in a privy James II came too near his favourite cannon. James III died at the hands of a court faction, aided by his son James IV who wore a chain of repentance for the rest of his life. The same James IV was a Renaissance king in high style who led the Scots to archetypal defeat at Flodden. James V was another proud king, yet he moved among his people in disguise. After another crushing defeat at Solway Moss, he received the news of his daughter's birth with an epitaph on his royal line – *It cam wi a lass and it'll gang wi a lass* – and turned his face to the wall. Mary the lass, however, lived to become the most famous of all Scots monarchs, albeit one with a talent for losing husbands, her throne and finally her head. James VI, her only son, was labelled the 'wisest fule in Christendom' by his Presbyterian opponents, but cannily lived on to rule Scotland, England and Ireland and to inspire Shakespeare's *Macbeth*. Charles I emulated his grandmother by losing his throne and head, while Charles II displayed courage in adversity and indulgence in prosperity. James VII threw away the throne for religion and fathered the Jacobite Pretenders. Bonnie Prince Charlie gambled the loyalty of Scotland – Highland and, to some extent, Lowland – to recover his throne. After dancing at Holyrood and marching to Derby, he looked on helpless as the independent power and culture of the Highland clans was brutally broken at Culloden.

The early parts of this saga are worked up for general consumption in the racy sixteenth-century chronicle of Lyndsay of Pitscottie.[36] 'Auld Pitscottie's' account of James III's tragedy is a masterly slow development of fatal outcomes from fatal flaws. Overdependent on favourites, James's suspicious mind is poisoned, according to Pitscottie, by a witch who prophesies 'that he should be suddenlie slain with ane of the neirest of his kin'. This leads to the murder of one royal brother and to the condemnation and dramatic escape of another. However, the witch appears to have been a tool of James's favourite Cochran, who now lords it over the Scottish court till, in typical political mode, the Scottish aristocracy hang him and his associates from Lauder Brig. Faction follows faction till James's son and heir agrees to join an army against his father. Before the subsequent battle at

Sauchie near Stirling, James remembers the prophecy of the witch which he – and we – now realise applies to his own son and not his dead or exiled brothers. He turns to flee alone, is thrown by his horse and taken, unrecognised, into the Mill at Bannockburn. Recovering his senses, he asks for a priest and tells the miller's wife that he is the king. She 'cryit for ane priest to the king' and an unidentified enemy pretending to be a priest gains entry, kneels by the king's bed and, on being asked for confession and communion, 'gif him foure or five straiks ewin to the heart'. Local tradition identifies James Striveling of Keir as the assassin. So James IV came to the throne of Scotland.[37]

Violence and treachery are often catalysts in the historical stories. If Barbour's *Bruce* depicts an ideal knightly partnership between Sir James Douglas and his King, then Pitscottie traces a remorseless and bloody trail of plot, counter-plot and feud between the Stewart monarchs and the Douglas earls. This material, however, is leavened in popular tradition by love interest, not least on the parts of James IV and V. As a young man, James IV fell deeply in love with Margaret Drummond but the match was opposed by the nobility who wanted a politically advantageous marriage. James, however, was already secretly promised to Margaret who gave birth to a daughter and, while Margaret lived, James would not consider another marriage, even if she could not be his queen. In 1501, Margaret and her two sisters died after eating together and poison was widely suspected. The three sisters were buried together in the Choir of Dunblane Cathedral and a year later James was betrothed to Princess Margaret of England, so uniting the thistle and the rose. An anonymous poem, 'By Tayis Bank the Rose Blumes Bricht',[38] celebrating Margaret Drummond's beauty, has been ascribed to James who had daily masses said for her soul till the end of his life. The story of James's romance and its denouement survived the king's later amours because it is a tale of tragic death and true love tragically thwarted.

Tradition has James V pursuing more low life adventures in his guise as the Gaberlunzie man or, in other less amorous tales, as the Gudeman o Ballengeich. The point of these stories lies in the revelation of the king's identity on a subsequent occasion and the reward of those who have rendered the Gudeman some service. The king disguised is a folk tale motif also favoured in Romance narratives and satirised in 'The Colkelbie Sow'. The lover who conceals his identity but turns out to be high-born is also a motif favoured in Scottish ballads such as 'The Gaberlunzie Man' and 'The Jolly Beggar'.[39] In variations on this theme the man and woman both turn out to be high-born. Or the woman turns out to be high-born and the man is a commoner – 'he was only the blacksmith's son'.

In Lowland Scots, storytelling material moved easily between history, folk tale and sung ballad because the sources of interest in each genre overlapped and oral tradition was a more effective and widespread medium than the minority culture of books and manuscripts. Ballads, therefore, could be either romantic or historical in interest, or a combination of the two. 'Sir Patrick Spens' seems to be one of the oldest surviving historical ballads and may be about the convoy which took Princess Margaret, Alexander III's only daughter, to marry King Eric of Norway. The brooding fatalism which dominates the ballad has also, however, been attached to later events when Margaret's daughter, the maid of Norway, died in transit to Scotland so setting in train the disasters of the inter-regnum:

> Late, late yestreen I saw the new moone
> Wi the auld moone in hir arme;
> And I feir, I feir, my dear master
> That we will com to harme.[40]

The Border ballads relate many historical events, such as the Battle of Otterburn and the hanging of Johnnie Armstrong, and they display a keen sense of locality. But the tone and purpose of these two examples is quite different. Otterburn is a celebration of chivalric bravery in the old Romance style, while the poem of Johnnie Armstrong condemns James IV for outright treachery and depicts the reiving Borderer as a Scottish hero.

John murdered was at Carlenrigg
And all his galant companie
But Scotland's heart was never sae wae
To see sae mony brave men die.[41]

I say poet because, though both ballads are formed to be orally sung and remembered, they are the work of individual artists and not a succession of anonymous folk singers. This is related in a controlling fidelity to an event, a place and specific personalities.

The same is true of another well-known historical ballad, 'The Bonnie Earl o Murray' which has been cunningly contrived as a piece of popular propaganda, memorable and catching. The poet's cause is the murder of the Bonnie Earl by the Earl of Huntly with the possible collusion of James VI. Huntly is accused and the King's excuses satirised with an attributed quote – 'I bade you bring him wi you/But forbade you him to slae'. Sexual jealousy is also imputed to James – 'And the Bonnie Earl of Murray/Oh he was the Queen's love'. Overall the ballad is a trumpet summons to the popular Protestant party to rise up and demand justice for its slain hero:

Ye Hielans and ye Lowlands
Oh where hae ye been
They hae slain the Earl of Murray
And hae laid him on the green.[42]

The Romance ballads have already been cited through 'Tam Lin' and 'Thomas the Rhymer', but the corpus as a whole is a powerful compendium of love, death and the supernatural. The strength of these ballads lies in their capacity for subtle variation within a set of motifs and story lines. The Romance ballads were and are sung by a large number of artists each of which remains loyal to their sources and their personal versions. The narratives are very direct and spare, setting the tale immediately in motion with clear dramatic action, vivid imagery and a physical sense of the value of every word and phrase. The narrative voice is impersonal but can move in and out of other dramatic voices in dialogue verses which are sometimes quite oblique and compressed. The ballad melody both sustains the flow and provides a constant ground against which the quality of the language can be concentrated, extended or manipulated to surprising effect. In the charge of a first class singer, the Lowland Scots ballad is high art in folk form and the ballad should be heard rather than read. Quotation, therefore, hardly suffices but a few classic openings give the characteristic flavour.

> Why does your brand sae drap wi bluid, Edward, Edward?
> Why does your brand sae drap wi bluid
> And why sae sad gang ye?
>
> (Edward, Edward)[43]

> There was a shepherd's dochter
> Kept sheep on yonder hill
> There cam a knicht o courage bricht
> And he wad hae his will
>
> (The Shepherd's Dochter)[44]

> There lived a wife at Usher's Well
> And a wealthy wife was she;
> She had three stout and stalwart sons
> And sent them oer the sea
>
> (The Wife of Usher's Well)[45]

> She sat down below a thorn
> Fine flowers in the valley;
> And there she has her sweet babe born
> And the green leaves they grow rarely
>
> (The Cruel Mother)[46]

> There were two sisters sat in a bower,
> Binnorie, O Binnorie,
> There came a knight to be their wooer,
> By the bonny Milldams of Binnorie
>
> (The Cruel Sister)[47]

We may be heading for murder, passion, rape, suicide or supernatural visitation, but the narrative gaze will be un-flinching.

Despite his sometimes patronising tone about folk artists and audiences, Sir Walter Scott was an enthusiastic collector of balladry which he brought together in his *Minstrelsy of the Scottish Border,* divided into sections of Historical Ballads, Romantic Ballads and Imitation Ballads. In comparison with oral ballads, Scott's own poetry and the imitations are thin gruel because they are linguistically and metrically smoothed out for the book-buying public. In his *Private Memoirs* James Hogg relates an encounter between the ballad-collecting Laird of Abbotsford – the Shirra – and his ballad-singing mother which makes exactly this point from the mouth of someone who had cause to know:

One fine day in the summer of 1801, as I was busily engaged working in the field at Ettrick House, Wat Shiel came over to me and said, that 'I boud gang away down to the Ramsey-cleuch as fast as my feet could carry me, for there war some gentlemen there wha wantit to speak to me.'

'Wha can be at the Ramseycleuch that want me, Wat?'

'I couldna say, for it wasna me that they spak to i' the byganging. But I'm thinking it's the Shirra an' some o' his gang.'

I was rejoiced to hear this for I had seen the first volumes of the Minstrelsy of the Scottish Border and had copied a number of old ballads from my mother's recital and sent them to the editor preparatory for a third volume. I accord-ingly went towards home to put on my Sunday clothes but, before reaching it, I met with THE SHIRRA and Mr. William Laidlaw coming to visit me. They alighted and remained in our cottage for a space better than an hour, and my mother chanted the ballad of Old Maitlan' to them, with which Mr. Scott was highly delighted. I had sent him a copy (not a very perfect one, as I found afterwards, from the singing of another Laidlaw) but I thought Mr. Scott had some dread of a part being forged, that had been the cause of his journey into the wilds of Ettrick. When he heard my mother sing it he was quite satisfied and I remember he asked her if she thought it had ever been printed; and her answer was, 'Oo, na, na, sir, it was never printed i' the world for my brothers an' me learned it frae auld Andrew Moor, an' he learned it, an' mony mair, frae auld Baby Mettlin, that was housekeeper to the first Laird o' Tushilaw.'

'That must be a very auld story indeed, Margaret,' said he.

'Ay it is that! It is an auld story! But mair nor that, except George Warton and James Steward, there was never ane o' my sangs prentit till ye prentit them yourself, an' ye hae spoilt them a'thegither. They war made for singing an' no for reading; and they're nouther right spelled nor right setten down.'[48]

Scott was to find his own voice in prose but, as this extract shows, he did make a significant contribution to an ingathering of oral traditions at a time when Scottish society was experiencing rapid change. Consideration of his history-making and prose fiction belongs to another chapter.

The synthesis and conclusion of this period, when balladry, folk tale, Romance and literary poetry interacted on each other, is to be found not in Scott but in Robert Burns's 'Tam o' Shanter'. Written in 1790, 'Tam o' Shanter' is a one-off in Burns's genre and belongs to a late period in the poet's development when his energies were primarily devoted to the collection of Scottish folk songs. 'Tam' is a narrative masterpiece but also something of a throw-back to the period of the Renaissance makars. It is inspired by the tales of Betty Davidson in his childhood, an extended reflection on folk traditions and a reading of Gavin Douglas's translation of the *Aeneid*.[49]

The process by which Burns came to write 'Tam o' Shanter' is unusually transparent, since, earlier in 1790, he writes a long letter in response to the enquiries of an antiquary, Captain Francis Grose, who had visited the poet in Dumfries.

Among the many Witch Stories I have heard relating to Aloway Kirk, I distinctly remember only two or three.

Upon a stormy night amid whirling squalls of wind and bitter blasts of air, in short on such a night as the devil would chuse to take the air in, a farmer or a farmer's servant was plodding and plashing homeward with his plough-irons on his shoulder, having been getting some repairs on them at a neighbouring smithy. His way lay by the Kirk of Aloway and, being rather on the anxious look-out in approaching a place so well known to be a favourite haunt of the devil and the devil's friends and emissaries, he was struck aghast by discovering, through the horrors of the storm and stormy night, a light which on his nearer approach plainly shewed itself to proceed from the haunted edifice. Whether he had been fortified from above on his devout supplication, as is customary with people when they suspect the immediate presence of Satan; or whether, according to another custom, he had got courageously drunk at the smithy, I will not pretend to determine; but so it was that he ventured to go up to, nay into the very Kirk. As good luck would have it, his temerity came off unpunished. The members of the infernal junto were all out on some midnight business or other and he saw nothing but a kind of kettle or caldron, depending from the roof, over the fire, simmering some heads of unchristened children, limbs of executed malefactors etc for the business of the night. It was in for a penny in for a poun, with the honest ploughman; so without ceremony he unhooked the caldron from off the fire and, pouring out the damnable ingredients, inverted it on his head, and carried it fairly home, where it remained long in the family a living evidence of the truth of the story.

Another story, which I can prove to be equally authentic, was as follows.

On a market in the town of Ayr a farmer from Carrick consequently whose way lay by the very gate of Aloway kirkyard, in order to cross the river Doon at the old bridge, which is about two or three hundred yards further on than the said gate, had been detained by his business till by the time he reached Aloway it was the wizard hour, between night and morning.

Though he was terrified with a blaze streaming from the

kirk, yet as it is a well known fact, that to turn back on these occasions is running by far the greatest risk of mischief, he prudently advanced on his road. When he had reached the gate of the kirk-yard he was surprised and entertained through the ribs and arches of an old gothic window which still faces the highway to see a dance of witches merrily footing it round their old sooty blackguard master, who was keeping them all alive with the power of his bagpipe. The farmer stopping his horse to observe them a little could plainly descry the faces of many old women of his acquaintance and neighbourhood. How the gentleman was dressed, tradition does not say; but the ladies were all in their smocks; and one of them happening unluckily to have a smock which was considerably too short to answer all the purpose of that piece of dress, our farmer was so tickled that he involuntarily burst out with a loud laugh, 'Weel luppen, Maggy wi' the short sark!' and, recollecting himself, instantly spurred his horse to the top of his speed. I need not mention the universally known fact that no diabolical power can pursue you beyond the middle of a running stream. Lucky it was for the poor farmer that the river Doon was so near, for notwithstanding the speed of his horse, which was a good one, against he reached the middle of the arch of the bridge and consequently the middle of the stream, the pursuing, vengeful hags were so close at his heels that one of them actually sprung to seize him: but it was too late; nothing was on her side of the stream but the horse's tail, which immediately gave way to her infernal grip, as if blasted by a stroke of lightning; but the farmer was beyond her reach. However, the unsightly, tailless condition of the vigorous steed was, to the last hours of the noble creature's life, an awful warning to the Carrick farmers not to stay too late in Ayr markets.[50]

Here, clearly, are the immediate narrative sources which later that year went into, 'Tam o' Shanter'. But two further ingredients were required. There is a dramatic contrast between the distancing Enlightenment prose of the Grose letter and the virile Scots of the poem – could the same person have written both? The answer is 'yes', because the achievement of 'Tam' is to blend the mock heroic mode of classical literature with Scots folk tale. 'Honest Tam' is the low life descendant of Virgil's 'pious Aeneas'.

At the same time, Tam, like Thomas the Rhymer before him, is making a mythic journey of descent into the other-world of magic and witchcraft but, unlike the heroes of Romance, he is sent packing with his tail cropped, back to the role of hen-pecked husband, adumbrated at the start:

> Oh Tam, hadst thou but been sae wise
> As taen thy ain wife Kate's advice
> She tauld thee weel thou was a skellum
> A blethering, blustering, drunken blellum.[51]

The mock heroic parallel to this is the narrator's expostula-tion to the 'gentle dames' who deliver such 'counsels sweet':

> Ah, gentle dames! It gars me greet
> To think how many counsels sweet
> How many lengthen'd sage advices
> The husband frae the wife despises.[52]

In 'Tam o' Shanter', Burns also appeals to a distinctively Scottish genre of poetry – the poems of folk festivity. This category covers exuberant verse accounts of plays, fairs, weddings, races and even Presbyterian Communion Seasons (notably in Burns' own 'The Holy Fair').[53] The scene which Tam encounters in Alloway Kirkyard is a folk festivity but populated by the dead enjoying a witches' Sabbath under the musical direction of the Devil himself. At least someone in Scottish society still knew how to enjoy life! Note, though how the communion table, the 'haly table', is adorned for this particularly Unholy Fair:

> Inspiring bold John Barleycorn!
> What dangers thou canst make us scorn!
> Wi' tippeny we fear nae evil;
> Wi' usquabae, we'll face the devil!

The swats sae ream'd in Tammie's noddle,
Fair play, he car'd na deils a boddle.
But Maggie stood right sair astonish'd,
Till, by the heel and hand admonish'd,
She ventured forward on the light;
And, vow! Tam saw an unco sight!
Warlocks and witches in a dance;
Nae cotillion brent new frae France,
But hornpipes, jigs, strathspeys and reels,
Put life and mettle in their heels.
A winnock-bunker in the east,
There sat auld Nick in shape o' beast;
A towzie tyke, black, grim and large,
To gie them music was his charge:
He screw'd the pipes and gart them skirl,
Till roof and rafters a' did dirl –
Coffins stood round, like open presses,
That shaw'd the dead in their last dresses;
And by some devilish cantraip slight
Each in its cauld hand held a light –
By which heroic Tam was able
To note upon the haly table,
A murderer's banes in gibbet airns;
Twa span-lang, wee unchristen'd bairns;
A thief, new-cutted frae a rape,
Wi' his last gasp his gab did gape;
Five tomahawks, wi' blude red-crusted
Five scymitars, wi' murder crusted;
A garter, which a babe had strangled;
A knife, a father's throat had mangled,
Whom his ain son o' life bereft,
The grey hairs yet stack to the heft;
Wi' mair o' horrible and awefu',
Which even to name wad be unlawfu'.
As Tammie glow'rd, amaz'd, and curious,
The mirth and fun grew fast and furious:
The piper loud and louder blew;
The dancers quick and quicker flew;
They reel'd, they set, they cross'd, they cleekit,

Till ilka carlin swat and reekit,
And coost her duddies to the wark,
And linket at it in her sark![54]

Tam cannot restrain his role to that of voyeur, not least in the case of Cutty Sark. 'Weel done, Cutty Sark!' he yells and the fury of the witch – or is it the fairy? – host is turned on the mortal interloper. The hero escapes over running water but leaves behind his ain grey mare Meg's tail: 'the carlin caught her by the rump/And left poor Maggie scarce a stump'. Back Tam limps to the world of Kirk Sessions, markets, honest labour and nagging wives, leaving some part of his essential self behind. Relations with the mother goddess and her witch/maidens seem to have got even more difficult since the time of Thomas the Rhymer!

Perhaps this reflects what Burns himself felt about the repressive economic and social order which the eighteenth century and the start of the Industrial Revolution had produced. One interpretation of the poem by a modern poet links 'Tam o' Shanter' with Tam the Chanter or poet: he is, in fact, another Thomas the Rhymer, inspired by John Barleycorn and 'crooning o'er some auld Scots sonnet'.[55] Certainly no one after Burns was again to possess the imaginative territory in which Romance, folk tales, balladry and literary poetry merge with such assurance. Three centuries of Scottish culture are encapsulated in Burns's 'Tam o' Shanter', but the world he evokes had to a large extent passed into history. Nonetheless, the narrative lives on and is still frequently recited from memory, not least at those ritual occasions called Burns Suppers.

Notes

1. For the cultural background to this period see Owen, D. D. R. (1997), *William the Lion: Kingship and Culture 1143–1214*, East Lothian: Tuckwell Press.
2. Ibid. p. 28.
3. See Gowans, Linda (1992), *Am Bron Binn: An Arthurian Ballad in Scottish Gaelic*, Eastbourne: Linda Gowans.
4. See Johannis de Fordun, *Chronica Gentis Scotonum*, ed. William

F. Skene (1871), Edinburgh: Edmonston & Douglas, pp. xxxviii–xxxix and p. 207.

5. See Stewart, Marion, 'King Orpheus' in *Scottish Studies*, Vol. 17, Part One, (1973), Edinburgh: School of Scottish Studies, pp. 1–16.

6. See Purser, John (1992), *Scotland's Music*, Edinburgh: Mainstream.

7. See *Sir Tristrem*, ed. George P. McNeill (1996), Edinburgh: Scottish Text Society, pp. xxv–xxxix.

8. *The Romance and Prophecies of Thomas of Erceldoune*, ed. James A. H. Murray (1875), London: Early English Text Society, pp. 2–3

9. Kinsley, James (ed.) (1969), *The Oxford Book of Ballads*, Oxford: Oxford University Press, p. 7.

10. Scott, Sir Walter, 'Introductory Remarks on Popular Poetry', p. 14 in *Sir Walter Scott Minstrelsy of the Scottish Border* (1932), Vol. I, ed. T. F. Henderson, Edinburgh: Oliver & Boyd.

11. *The Oxford Book of Ballads*, p. 7.

12. See Moffat, Alistair (1999), *Arthur and the Lost Kingdoms*, London: Weidenfield and Nicolson, passim.

13. See Clancy, Thomas Owen (1998), *The Triumph Tree: Scotland's Earliest Poetry AD 550–1350*, Edinburgh: Canongate Books, pp. 46–78.

14. *Scotland's Music*, p. 66.

15. *The Romance and Prophecies of Thomas of Erceldoune*, p. 14.

16. *The Triumph Tree: Scotland's Earliest Poetry AD 550–1350*, p. 297.

17. For the most accessible edition of the text with introduction see Barbour, John, *The Bruce*, ed. Duncan, A. A. M. (1997), Edinburgh: Canongate Books. For suggestions of ballad influence on *The Bruce*, see Henderson, Hamish, 'The Ballad and Popular Tradition to 1660' in Craig, Cairns (ed.) (1988), *The History of Scottish Literature* Vol. I, ed. R. D. S. Jack, Aberdeen: Aberdeen University Press, pp. 263–4.

18. *The Bruce*, pp. 459–61.

19. See *Hary's Wallace*, ed. Matthew P. McDiarmid (1968), Vol. I, Edinburgh: Scottish Text Society, pp. xv–xxv.

20. Ibid. pp. xxxviii–xlviii.

21. See Brown , J. T. T. (1900) *The Wallace and The Bruce Restudied*, Bonn: P. Hoenstein's Verlag, pp. 7–10.

22. *Hary's Wallace*, pp. xxviii–xxix.

23. See *Scottish Poetry from Barbour to James VI*, ed. M. M. Gray (1935), London: J.M. Dent.

24. See *Longer Scottish Poems*, Vol. I, ed. Priscilla Bawcutt and Felicity Riddy (1987), Edinburgh: Scottish Academic Press: Edinburgh, pp. 171–2.
25. Ibid. pp. 94–133.
26. For a general summary of this literature, see McDiarmid, M. P. 'The Metrical Chronicles and Non-alliterative Romances' in Cairns Craig (ed.), *The History of Scottish Literature* Vol. I, 'Origins to 1660', ed. R. D. S. Jack, pp. 27–38.
27. See *The Complaynt of Scotland*, ed. A. M. Stewart (1979), Edinburgh: Scottish Text Society, p. 25. This work is normally attributed to Robert Wedderburn but its authorship is uncertain.
28. See *The Poetry of Scotland*, ed. Roderick Watson(1995), Edinburgh: Edinburgh University Press, pp. 137–43.
29. *A Forgotten Heritage: Original Folk Tales of Lowland Scotland* edited by Aitken, Hannah (1973), Edinburgh: Scottish Academic Press, p. 94.
30. Ibid. p. 95.
31. Ibid. pp. 114–17 and p. 73.
32. Ibid. pp. 63–4.
33. Ibid. p. 77.
34. Ibid. p. 86.
35. Ibid. p. 61.
36. See Robert Lindsay of Pitscottie, *Historie and Cronicles of Scotland*, Vols I and II, ed. A. E. J. G. Mackay (1894), Edinburgh: William Blackwell & Sons.
37. Ibid. Vol. II, pp. 208–9.
38. See *Ballatis of Luve*, ed. John MacQueen (1970), Edinburgh: Edinburgh University Press, pp. 44–50. MacQueen accepts that the poem is for Margaret Drummond but questions the legend that James had set his heart on marrying her. However, the Drummond family tradition is definite on this point.

Margaret Drummond, eldest daughter of John Lord Drummond, was a lady of rare perfections and singular beautie. With her, the young King James the 4th was [so] deeply enamoured, that without acquainting his Nobles or Council, he was affianced to her in order to have made her his Queen. But so soon as his intentions were discovered, all possible obstructions were made both by the Nobility, who designed an allyance with a daughter of England as a mean to procure Peace betwixt the Nations, and by the Clergie, who declared against the lawfulness of the marriage, because they were within the degrees of consanguinity, forbidden by the Canon Law. Nevertheless, the King, under promise, gott her with child, which proved a daughter, [in the year 1497] and was called lady Margaret Stewart; but he was so much touched in conscience for the engagement he had made to the young Lady, that, notwithstanding the weakness of the Royal family, he rejected all propositions of marriage, so long as she lived: for he was crowned in the year 1488, at the age of sixteen, and did not marry untill the year 1502, when he was near thirty, and about a year after her death, which was effected not without suspicion of poyson, for the common tradition goes, that a potion was provided in a breakfast to dispatch her for liberating the King from his promise, that he might match with England; but it happened that she called two of her sisters, then with her, lady Flemyng and a younger [sister] Sybilla, a maid, whereby it fell out all the three were destroyed with the force of the poyson. They ly buried in a curious vault, covered with 3 fair blue marble stones joined closs together, about the middle of the quyre of the Cathedral church of Dumblane: for about this time the buriall place for the family of Drummond at Innerpaffray was not yet built. The Monument which contains the ashes of these three ladys stands intire to this day, and confirms the credit of this sad story.

From *History of the Family of Drummond*, [by William Viscount of Strathallan] 1681. MS folio 188 Drumm Castle.

39. See *The Oxford Book of Ballads* pp. 624–9.
40. Ibid. p. 312.
41. Ibid. p. 524.
42. Ibid. p. 594. For discussion of the political significance of this ballad, see Cowan, Edward J. 'Calvinism and the Survival of Folk' in *The People's Past*, ed. Edward J. Cowan (1980), Edinburgh: EUSPB, pp. 32–57
43. Ibid. p. 239.
44. Ibid. p. 263.
45. Ibid. p. 94.
46. Ibid. p. 68.
47. Ibid. p. 69.
48 Hogg, James, *Memoirs of the Author's Life and Familiar Anecdotes of Sir Walter Scott*, ed. Douglas G. Mack (1972), Edinburgh: Scottish Academic Press, pp. 61–2.

49. See MacQueen, John (1982), *Progress and Poetry: The Enlight-
    enment and Scottish Literature* Vol. I, Edinburgh: Scottish Aca-
    demic Press, pp. 134–54, for seminal and authoritative
    exposition of the poem.
50. Ibid. pp. 136–7.
51. Burns, *Poems and Songs*, ed. James Kinsley (1971), Oxford:
    Oxford University Press, p. 443.
52. Ibid. p. 50.
53. For a discussion and edited selection of this genre, see *The
    Christis Kirk Tradition: Scots Poems of Folk Festivity*, ed. Allen H.
    MacLaine (1996), Glasgow: Association for Scottish Literary
    Studies.
54. Burns, *Poems and Songs*, p. 446.
55. See White, Kenneth, 'Tam O'Shanter: an Interpretation' in
    Scottish Literary Journal Vol. 17 No. 2 (November, 1990),
    pp. 5–15.

Making Sense?

◆

The main motivation of collectors is the fear that something may be lost. The belief that the society which had sustained oral narrative in folk tale, legend and ballad was fast disappearing is common to Robert Burns, Sir Walter Scott, Allan Cunningham, James Hogg, Peter Buchan, Robert Chambers and many others who devoted considerable energy to gathering and interpreting Scotland's oral traditions at the end of the eighteenth and the beginning of the nineteenth centuries. The same motivation possessed Campbell of Islay and his collectors in the Highlands a few decades later.

It is during this same period that industrialisation, urbanisation, migration, emigration and clearance began to severely disrupt the stability of Scottish social life, dispersing families and communities. What effect did this have on oral memory, and what part did oral tradition play in evaluating and handing on the human experience of these changes at the receiving end? How did Scotland's story makers make sense of what was happening, and was overall understanding of Scotland's master narratives contested or reshaped?

As the nineteenth century proceeds, the gap between the collector and his sources increased both socially and in mental attitude. Burns is operating so close to communal tradition that he – and we three centuries later – can barely distinguish between collection, recreation and invention in his lyric songs or in a ballad such as 'John Barleycorn'.[1] As an intellectual writer James Hogg is at one remove from the oral balladry of his mother, but he is not socially alienated from her community and sympathises with many of its beliefs and values, not least folk tradition's sense of the supernatural or spiritual. Sir Walter Scott, by contrast, is a product of the Edinburgh Enlightenment who self-consciously re-identifies with the traditions of his ancestors and skilfully turns them into literary art and commercial success. At the same time, as we have seen, Scott can be patronising about folk culture and, in life and politics, the Laird of Abbotsford did everything in his power to oppose the onset of democracy and to sustain inherited privilege.

This mental and social gap is well illustrated by the story of Robert Chambers.[2] Robert and his brother William were brought up in the Scots-speaking Borders town of Peebles but, following the failure of their father's small-scale water-powered textile manufacture, they walked to Edinburgh and set up as booksellers, living in poverty behind their Leith Walk stall, with one set of clothes apiece. Following in Scott's commercial footsteps, they courageously moved into publishing, beginning with a Scott-inspired monograph on the Border Gypsies. The brothers Chambers went on to become epitomes of Victorian Enlightenment and Industry creating a publishing empire, dictionaries, periodicals and encyclopaedias. William Chambers also became, as Lord Provost of Edinburgh, a major Victorian improver – commemorated in Chambers Street – but he also demonstrated his love of Scotland's heritage by personally financing the restoration of St Giles' Cathedral.

Robert Chambers was the author and historian of the two brothers. Following in Scott's footsteps, he produced a book about the real-life originals of characters in the *Waverley* novels, an excellent history of the Jacobite Risings, a biography of Burns and a popular chronological collection of Scottish historical sources entitled *Domestic Annals of Scotland* (1859).[3] One of Chambers' earliest works, *Traditions of Edinburgh* (1826), is a gathering of oral traditions and popular lore about Edinburgh's Old Town, so it is hardly surprising that at some time he should source the oral culture of his Borders boyhood:

Reared amidst friends to whom popular poetry furnished a daily enjoyment, and led by a tendency of my own mind to

delight in whatever is quaint, whimsical, and old, I formed
the wish, at an early period of life, to complete, as I
considered it, the collection of the traditionary verse of
Scotland, by gathering together and publishing all that
remained of a multitude of rhymes and short snatches of
verse applicable to places, families, natural objects, amusements, etc, wherewith, not less than by song and ballad, the
cottage fireside was amused in days gone past, while yet
printed books were only familiar to comparatively few. This
task was executed as well as circumstances would permit, and
a portion of the Popular Rhymes of Scotland was published
in 1826. Other objects have since occupied me, generally of
a graver kind; yet, amidst them all, I have never lost my wish
to complete the publication of these relics of the old natural
literature of my native country.[4]

This introduction belongs to the 1841 edition of Chambers' *Popular Rhymes of Scotland* and may reflect a greater
distance between the established Victorian man of letters
and the Peebles boy than applied to the young writer of
1826, though, as Chambers indicates, he went on adding to
the material with each edition. Given the literary and dramatic quality of Chambers' collected folk tales, as encountered in the previous chapter, and the inherent interest of
the rhymes and poems, as well as Chambers' superb commentary on them, the tone of the defensive apology with
which he continues is remarkable:

I cannot help feeling anxious that the articles collected may
be viewed in a proper light. It is to be observed, first of all,
that they are, in most instances, the production of rustic wits,
in some of the whimsies of mere children, and originally
were designed for no higher purpose than to convey the
wisdom or the humours of the cottage, to soothe the
murmurs of the cradle, or enliven the sports of the village
green. The reader is therefore not to expect here anything
profound, or sublime, or elegant, or affecting. But if he can
so far upon occasion undo his mature man, as to enter again
into the almost meaningless frolics of children – if to him the

absence of high-wrought literary grace is compensated by a simplicity coming direct from nature – if to him there be a poetry in the very consideration that such a thing, though a trifle, was perhaps the same trifle to many human beings like himself hundreds of years ago, and has, times without number, been trilled or chanted by hearts light as his own, long since resolved into dust – then it is possible that he may find something in this volume which he will consider worthy of his attention.[5]

There is clearly an element of authorial affectation here but it masks a genuine unease, not just about the reader's evaluation or interest, but the author's as well. Culture had become an issue of social class and the Victorian middle classes, who dominated official Scottish culture, were hostile to Scots oral tradition, since it was seen as rude (that is, impolite) and low class. The best Chambers could hope for is that Victorian middle class readers might indulge his taste for the surviving treasures of a vigorous, frank, egalitarian culture on the grounds that they were the 'whimsies of mere children' and 'meaningless frolics'.

The cultural paradox implicit in Chambers excusing his interest and simultaneously devoting energy and imagination to his collecting points to the deeper problem of social discontinuity and disruption in Scotland. Between the 1780s and the mid-nineteenth century, agricultural improvements, industrialisation, economic migration, clearance and urbanisation caused, sometimes within one generation, the most drastic movement of population and the most far-reaching changes ever experienced in Scottish social life. This economically driven dislocation set the pattern of greater mobility for future generations but, during these upheavals, there was no political protection outside wealth or privilege, and very little physical or psychological relief for the many victims.

Yet, despite these huge changes and their sometimes life-threatening consequences, we know relatively little of those who were at the sharp edge. This is because the social and community context which sustains oral tradition was often lost, leaving people no means by which to express their humanity within this situation or to pass on their experience. It is a cruel irony, for example, that, in some cases, the only surviving information about the clearance of a whole Highland glen or community is in the unemotive records of the estate managers who drove the process. The breaking of the ceilidh house as the centre of Gaelic hospitality and community, known as *duthchas*, also disrupted the continuity of memory and tradition – *dualchas*. Cultural deprivation, therefore, became one more oppression to add to the environmental degradation and physical pressures leading to demoralisation and disease amongst the urban and rural poor in the first half of the nineteenth century. However, the voices of these generations have been muffled rather than entirely silenced and the way in which their experience was, sometimes indirectly, transmitted became a potent factor in the politicisation of what came to be termed the working classes.

Firstly, the gradual spread of education gave talented working people access to the print media, both in book form and in chap books and broadsheets; as in previous periods, written forms reflected and interacted with the oral. Janet Hamilton was born at Langloan in Coatbridge in 1795. Her father was a shoemaker and she married his journeyman, giving birth to ten children. Although she attended school irregularly, her mother taught her to read and, when Janet was over fifty, she learned to write and began to produce poems and later essays. Janet Hamilton provides the rare witness of a working woman to the transformation of rural Lanarkshire into an industrial landscape:

> the weird fires of spunkie [Will-o'-the-wisp, marsh fires] glimmer and dance no more on the marsh, which is now lighted up by the lurid flames of iron smelting furnaces, and the sweet breath of the gowany and white clover lea is now exchanged for the stifling and sulphurous fumes arising from smouldering heaps of hot cinders and burning slag; and in place of the pale, indolent artizan basking on the green brae, and chanting some favourite Scotch ditty, we see

91

crowds of black, begrimed, sweating and toiling mortals at
the fires high and low, making the air vocal with 'the
frequent curse and the cheek-distending oath', and for
the songs of the birds and the music of the stream, we have
the scream of the locomotive and the never-ending clank of
machinery and grinding of wheels.[6]

Janet Hamilton was perhaps fortunate in being able to live
in the same place all her life. Shoemakers, like tailors and
blacksmiths, were known in the eighteenth century as re-
positories of tradition and Janet combines the approaches of
written and oral poetry to react to industrialisation's effect
on both the landscape and the community in a long poem
entitled 'A Wheen Aul' Memories':

Oot-owre the auld brig, up to sweet Simmerlee,
Sweet, said ye? – hech, whaur? – for nae sweetness I see;
Big lums spewin' reek an' red lowe on the air,
Steam snoring an' squellin', and whiles muckle mair!

Explodin' an' smashin' an' crashin', an' then
The wailin' o' women an' groanin' o men,
A' scowther't an' mangle't, sae painfu' to see –
The sweetness is gane, noo it's black Simmerlee.
[. . .]
The auld warl' dwallin' had a muckle clay brace,
An' lum whaur the stars glintit doun i' yer face
As ye sat by the fire; to the blue licht abune
Ye micht glower through the reek at the bonny hairst mune.

Noo the bodies are gane an' their dwallin's awa'
An' the place whaur they stood I scarce ken noo ava,
For there's roarin' o' steam an' there's reengin' o' wheels,
Men workin', an' sweatin', an' swearin' like deils.

An' the flame-tappit furnaces staun' in a raw,
A' bleezin' an' blawin' an' smeekin' awa'.
Their eerie licht brichtenin' the laigh hingin' cluds,
Gleamin far ower the loch an' the mirk lanely wuds.[7]

The twentieth-century poet and editor, Duncan Glen, uses the work of Janet Hamilton, in combination with parish records, modern economic history, industrial archaeology, and local knowledge, to provide a connected story of what happened to one representative Scottish community and its people in his *A Nation in Parish. A new historical prospect of Scotland from the parish of Cambuslang*. Glen makes this judgement about Janet Hamilton's work and its purpose:

> Janet Hamilton also saw long-established tradition swept away in the bright dawn of laissez-faire capitalism that shut out rising suns for many who moved from a rural society to that of urban slums. Unlike today's purveyors of nostalgia who yearn for a day, and a country, that never was, Janet Hamilton was no backward-looking sentimentalist; rather she was a realist who knew, had experienced, the social evils of both the old rural and the new industrial Lanarkshire. She was a true idealist, and looked to the new industries, properly organised and exploited, as a means of social and material improvement for the poor – to whom she dedicated her writings.[8]

Janet Hamilton's later written work depended for its wider outlets on publishers and the popular press, but more immediate reactions and protests were conveyed through chap books and broadsheet publications.

Alexander Wilson was born in 1766 and became an apprentice weaver in Paisley. In 1789, he travelled as a pedlar, writing and performing poems as he went along and collecting subscriptions for their publication. But Wilson was soon in trouble because of his broadsheet poems attacking specific manufacturers for cheating weavers and other honest workers. He was fined, later imprisoned and, finally, left for Philadelphia, though not before his humorous ballad 'Watty and Meg or The Wife Reformed' had sold a reputed 100,000 copies across Scotland. This kind of success reflects the power of popular poetry and its close relationship with communal tradition at the same time as Burns was a household name. Many in fact believed that the anonymously published Watty and Meg was by Burns himself.[9]

The weaver poets are a strong link between the written and the oral, and between rural and urban, since their message is often one of radical protest against contemporary conditions.[10] William Finlayson's 'Weavers' Lament', for example, is subtitled 'On the Failure of the Celebrated Strike of Weaving for a Minimum of Wages in 1812'. The weavers were also prominent in the radical political protests and risings of 1818–20 in Scotland which led to executions and transportations. One protest song from this period 'Jimmie Raeburn' also achieved mass circulation in broad-sheet form:

My name is Jimmie Raeburn, fae Glasgow toon I came;
My place and habitation I'm forced tae leave wi' shame;
From my place and habitation I now maun gang awa',
Far frae the bonnie hills and dales o' Caledonia.

It was early one morning, just by the break of day,
We were 'wakened by the turnkey, who unto us did say –
'Arise, ye hapless convicts, arise ye ane and a'.
This is the day ye are to stray from Caledonia.'

We all arose, put on our clothes, our hearts were full of grief,
Our friends who a' stood round the coach, could grant us no
    relief;
Our parents, wives, and sweethearts, their hearts were broke
    in twa,
To see us leave the hills and dales o' Caledonia.

Farewell, my aged mother, I'm vexed for what I've done,
I hope none will cast up to you the face that I have run;
I hope God will protect you when I am far awa,
Far from the bonnie hills and dales of Caledonia.

Farewell, my honest father, you are the best of men,
And likewise my own sweetheart, it's Catherine is her name,
Nae mair we'll walk by Clyde's clear stream or by the
    Broomielaw
For I must leave the hills and dales of Caledonia.[11]

94

The David Laing collection of broadsheet ballads, which was gathered in the early nineteenth century in Edinburgh, contains more than nine hundred items, and Jimmy Raeburn alone may have generated 100,000 copies.

This folk literature spread through performance and in printed form and was functional in the same way as rural folk song and folk tale had sustained the values of their communities. The weaver poets and broadsheet balladeers provide a vital link between older forms of popular culture and organisations such as the Chartist Movement and early trade unions, which eventually enabled urban and rural populations to regain some role in their own destiny and welfare. History, for a while, had deprived many folk of a narrative rooted in land, family and community, but gradually working people shaped a new historical aspiration or master narrative which found political and practical expression through socialism and the Labour movement. If what had been suffered made no sense, then perhaps the future would be shaped by justice and equality.

In the Highlands, this process took longer because the dislocation had, if anything, been more severe. But the threads of continuity were picked up and shaped in new ways. Again the poets provide some of our earliest glimpses. An anonymous writer produced this angry protest against the clearance between 1805 and 1810 of eighteen families from Arichanan in Argyll by Malcolm of Poltalloch:

> A wicked man is Malcolm
> And I will ever say it
> When the French come
> Across to rout him
> Who will stand up for Malcolm
> In the rabble round about him?
> Everyone will be wild
> Desiring to strike him
> And I myself will be there
> Urging on the conflict.[12]

95

A complementary note of lament is struck by John MacLachlan of Morvern in response to clearances in the 1820s:

> As I climb up towards Ben Shiant,
> my thoughts are filled with sadness
> seeing the mountain as a wilderness,
> with no cultivation on its surface.
> As I look down over the pass,
> what a chilling view I have!
> So many cottages in disarray,
> in green ruins on each side,
> and houses without a roof,
> in heaps by the water spring!
> Where the fire and children once were,
> That's where the rushes have grown tallest.[13]

Much information about the early clearances, however, is dependent on outside observers, such as the visiting journalist who recorded this incident in the Strath of Kildonan in Sutherland in 1820:

> On notice being given to these poor creatures to remove, they remonstrated and stated unequivocally that, as they neither had money to transport them to America nor the prospect of another situation to retire to, they neither could nor would remove and that, if force was to be used, they would rather die on the spot that gave them birth than elsewhere.[14]

In this as in many similar cases the landlords were able to call in the army to enforce their will.

However, the experience of clearance for all its devastation was tenaciously retained in oral tradition, both in Scotland and in Highland communities abroad, particularly those in places such as Nova Scotia which kept their Gaelic language and culture alive. Moreover, the physical remains of the dispossessed townships memorialised the Highland landscape, creating a new layer of *Dinnseanchas* or lore of place. When, in the 1880s, the Highland crofters began to organise their economic, cultural and political fight-back, the connection of the generations proved to have survived the cataclysm. The Royal Commission of 1883, set up to examine crofting grievances, recorded hundreds of oral testimonies like the evidence given by Malcolm McAskill, a crofter from near Dunvegan in Skye:

> I am 36 years of age and was born in Kilmuir, parish of Duirinish. My father was born as Ramasaig and is about 75 years of age. He was evicted from there to Idrigill, from Idrigill to Forse, and from Forse back to Idrigill, where he was only one year. Then he was removed to his present croft . . . He was removed from the first four places for no other reason than to make way for sheep. He was not in arrears of rent. He has seen all the following townships laid waste or depopulated: Lowergill, Ramasaig, Ollasdale, Dibidale, Idrigill, Forse, Varkasaig.[15]

Amidst the Gaelic poems and folk tales gathered by Alexander Carmichael in his *Carmina Gaedelica,* James Hunter, the leading contemporary historian of the Highlands, pinpoints this recollection of childhood recorded from an old woman in Lochboisdale in the 1870s or 1880s:

> How we enjoyed ourselves in those faraway days – the old as much as the young. I often saw three, and sometimes four, generations dancing together on the green grass in the golden summer sunset: men and women of fourscore or more – for they lived long in those days – dancing with boys and girls of five on the green grass. Those were happy days and happy nights, and there was neither sin nor sorrow in the world for us . . . But the clearances came upon us, destroying all, turning our joy into misery, our gladness into bitterness, our blessing into blasphemy, and our christianity into mockery. *O a dhuine ghaolaich, thig na deoir air mo shuilean le linn smaoininn air na dh'fhuilig sinn agus na duirbh thainig sinn roinhe!* Oh dear man, the tears come on my own eyes when I think of all we suffered and of the sorrows, hardships, oppressions we came through![16]

These words of Peggy McCormack are a strong oral parallel to the writings of Janet Hamilton and, like Duncan Glen, James Hunter stresses the realism of these memories in context:

> It is easy to respond to such sentiments by observing, quite correctly, that South Uist never was the earthly paradise Peggy McCormack believed it to have been, but that is wholly to miss the point she so eloquently made. During Peggy McCormack's lifetime there had been deliberately destroyed, both in South Uist and in much of the rest of the Highlands and Islands, socially cohesive and generally self-assured communities of the type she had been born into. In place of those communities, by the 1860s and 1870s, were congested collectives consisting for the most part of crofting families who, despite their having survived famine and clearance, had been so marginalised and so demoralised as to make it perfectly understandable that, for the greater part of the nineteenth century, no thought of taking on their landlords appears to have entered their heads.[17]

Even as Carmichael was recording Peggy McCormack's memories, the tide was beginning to turn and the spirit and eloquence with which she speaks is itself testimony to the survival of communal values. People who have been marginalised in the way Hunter describes may draw resources from the natural and spiritual worlds and demonstrate the way in which the human spirit can outface harsh reality. This is true of both rural and urban situations in today's economically driven global culture.

Popular broadsheets and journalism have been cited as ways in which the dislocated and displaced populations of early nineteenth-century Scotland registered their reaction and sustained their own culture and experience in new contexts. However, it was not until the publication, in 1986, of William Donaldson's book, *Popular Literature in Victorian Scotland*, that the huge role of the press in sustaining Scots storytelling, language and oral culture became apparent. Donaldson traces the rise of the Scottish press from a cottage industry in 1800 to a multi-million pound enterprise, with over 200 daily and weekly titles in 1900. But is was the hugely popular weekly titles, which bore a tidal stream of poetry, fiction, reminiscences, biographies, history, folk tale, legend, musicology and folk song through the Victorian century.[18] This material was rarely published in book form, specifically catered for working people and was often in Scots. The pioneer in the field was William Chambers' *Edinburgh Journal* which majored in the 1830s on short stories and poems, Scottish history and biography, and popular antiquities.

Unlike the later Kailyard school of popular Scottish fiction which was tailored to the English and expatriate as well as the home market, titles such as *The People's Journal, Aberdeen Weekly Free Press, The North Briton, The Caithness Courier* and *The Glasgow Clincher* were produced by and for Scotland's urban and rural communities and circulated in very large numbers from mid-century. The weekly press is often humorous and aims to entertain, but it is also radical in its attitudes and tone. The following is a typically pungent paragraph from *The People's Journal* by W. D. Latto (alias Tammas Bodkin), its leading writer.

> There is still a large class, however, whose means winna alloo them to edicate their families, hoo willin soever they may be to do sae, and their hard case is nane the less the direct result o' Mammon-worship, no on their pairt indeed, for they canna help themsel's, but on that o' their employers, wha wickedly screw doon their wark folk until they are in a wayr condition than that wherein oor first parent faund himself when driven oot o' Paradise, for he was only condemned to eat his bread in the sweat o' his face – no to sweat and starve baith at the same time as we see folk doin' noo-a-days.[19]

At its peak the *Journal* had a circulation of quarter of a million copies each week.

The same qualities of vivid language, humour and social intelligence are evident in the stories and serialised novels in the weekly press, so providing a direct link between the poetry and recorded folk tales of the eighteenth century and the literary renaissance of the twentieth. The aim was to produce locally rooted fiction with popular appeal so, naturally, the writers turned to folk tale and local traditions. Local colour was, however, developed and applied with fairly broad brush strokes of melodrama, featuring ghosts, divine vengeance, inheritance, love, murder and tragic death. Mistaken or hidden identities are common, with dramatic denouements a cardinal requirement of the genre. Such motifs, however, do not necessarily belie serious social and moral intentions. William Donaldson comments shrewdly on the 'resurrectionist' theme in popular fiction which was also prevalent in the oral traditions of the Scottish Travelling people.

> Graves and graveyards are very much part of the stock furniture of the popular fiction of the period due in part to the activities of grave-robbers or 'resurrectionists' as they were popularly known. This was an age of great public interest in medicine and in the improved anatomy training provided for students, either in the Universities or in the numerous private anatomical schools. Legitimate sources of bodies – executed felons and so on – could hardly keep up with demand, and the plundering of graves to supply the anatomical table became a widespread practice. Resurrectionism took such an extraordinary hold on the popular imagination and occasioned so many stories even after it had long fallen into disuse, that it clearly possessed important symbolic overtones for contemporaries. During a period of rapid social change the plundering of the kirkyard, that obvious source of inherited value, might well imply, amongst other things, the violation of culture, the severing of links between past and present, the cancellation of traditional obligations.[20]

The debt which these shorter fictions owe to oral tradition and folk tale is highlighted by an 1853 correspondent to *The People's Journal* who feels that entrants for the *Journal*'s competition are recycling and not inventing!

Sir, – Not very long ago it was the custom in the straths and glens of the Highlands of Perthshire, and likely in Forfarshire, for the young men and old to meet together in the long winter evenings for the purpose of entertaining each other in relating stories and talking about their common affairs. At those cheerful gatherings someone was called to relate some tale, and each in his turn was called upon for a song or a story for the amusement or instruction or the company. At the time I speak of books were not so plentiful as they are now, and the Gaelic was the language best understood in those glens. Some of the men were particularly gifted in inventing and minutely relating tales. *The People's Journal*, I find, has got hold of some of these tales, and published them in a new garb. No doubt they will appear original to many of your readers, and their new dress will make them pass tolerably well. 'The Rival Tailors' [a tailor tries to outwit a colleague but becomes the victim of his own disingenuousness] 'The Minister and the Pat' [about a clergyman obsessed by crockery] and 'The Tempter Tempted' [a minister adopts a stratagem to stop his beadle drinking], etc I heard my father relate many a time for the amusement of the youth. When a prize is awarded by the Editor of *The Journal*, I think originality should be a consideration.[21]

William Alexander, editor of the weekly *Aberdeen Free Press*, is well known as the author of the classic Scottish novel *Johnnie Gibb of Gushetneuk (1871)*. Yet much more of his fiction is hidden within the surviving archival copies of *The Weekly Free Press*. In these fictions Alexander confronts the contemporary issues of social and economic change but he also probes back two or three generations into the older patterns of rural society, bridging the gap of dislocation and discontinuity. *Ravenshowe and the Residenters Therein – Sketches of a Hamlet of the Olden Time* was published in two parts, in 1867 and 1868, and represents Alexander's first serious attempt to come to terms with the changes in the rural society of north-east Scotland. In *Ravenshowe*, he moves beyond a concern with family history and generational connection to analyse what he calls 'social economics'. As William Donaldson points out, this analysis drew on oral tradition and from primary and secondary historical source material:

> 'Ravenshowe' covers the period from the 1780s to the 1830s and it tells the story of Eppie Copland from early woman-hood until her death. When it opens she is a crofter's daughter in the Garioch, being courted by her father's ploughman Donald Cameron. The pair of them 'canna gree' and Donald goes to be a smuggler at Newburgh on the Aberdeenshire coast, the trade then being rife, owing to wartime restrictions and the unsettled nature of the times. He passes utterly beyond ken for ten years, although at no point is he more than twenty miles away. This is a point Alexander makes again and again during the course of the novel – the way technology and the physical environment shape not only the immediate life-style but the whole mental world of the community. These are the days before turnpike roads and an intricate rail network transformed the internal communications of the North-East: travelling is a laborious, risky and time-consuming business, and the outside world seems unimaginably remote. The idea of the sea haunts the imagination of this landlocked parish as a mystical and unchancy element, gateway to places with shifting barbaric names and fairly hotching with 'peerats' and other wild characters.[22]

The language of *Ravenshowe* is rich and idiomatic and makes no concessions to an English-speaking readership in a way that is typical of the weekly press:

> 'Aye' [says Donald]' . . . it was kittle aneuch wark to keep clear o' the gaugers. Ye ist hed to dee the best wi' wiles, or speed o' fit, an' whiles a' wudna' dee.'
> 'Wus ye ever fairly into their grips, Donal'?'
> 'No.o. Weel aw cudna say't a hed. I hed ance a bit o' a sharry wi' a soopei weeoor creatur't fesh the haill pack o' them doon aboot my lugs. We hed gotten a nice trauchtie o'

Hollan's rum in fan some sleumin' hed won oot aboot it; so we gat the keggies buriet ano' the san' an' let them lie there for sax ouks. The gaugers dakkert ilka hoose toon an roon, and ca'd up the bents an' breem-knowes as weel they micht, for it wus a' fell snug mair nor four fit doon amo' the fair sea san'. Aweel a' this wears ower; the bit luggerie wus awa aff the coast for ouks, an' they hed g' en't up for a bad job. So ae gloamin jist about Michael day, we wud tak oor Hollan's up to them't they belang't till – we kent brawly faur to tak them.'

'Oh ye hed the gin saul afore han' – hed ye?'

'Ye wud won'er man fa wud be pairtners i' the concern,' said Donald pursuing his narrative. 'So there's a mannie liv't oot the roadside, he'd newlins gotten a Moray cairtie wi' a timmer aixtree – there wus hardly onything but the creels gaenthan-a-days – he wud len's his horsie an's cairtie un'er cover, to ca' the kegs o'er the knowe, but wudna gae 'imsel', upo' nae accoont. I gets the horsie an' the cairtie, and sets oot – it was gweed meenlicht, but the lift owre cas'en wi' flichterin' bits o' cloods. Aweel, a' gaes on fine till aw'm in the road a gey piece, fan ane o' the wheels o' the cairtie began to skirl at ilka turn like the vera mischief.[23]

The survival of such narrative material and language in an accessible and widely distributed form is a useful corrective to the notion that a distinctive Scottish literature faded out in the mid-nineteenth century to be replaced by a nostalgic 'Kailyard' view of Scottish culture as quaint and rural. However, it remains true that, from the late eighteenth century, the print medium was growing in influence, and cultural prestige rested with written literature, philosophy and history in English. This was a result of the eighteenth-century Scottish Enlightenment which, in turn, built on the educational and social policies of the Scottish Reformation. In the nineteenth century, the wealth and the institutional means became available to disseminate book culture much more widely through the population.

Sir Walter Scott is a key figure in these developments since he was the literary heir of the Scottish Enlightenment who established himself, early in the nineteenth century, as

Scotland's most popular author and he was a pioneer in the large scale commercial publication of literature. But, for our purposes, it is Scott's invention or at least recreation of the historical novel and his interest in historiography that commands attention. While retaining the Enlightenment interest in universal human characteristics, Scott developed, imaginatively and perceptively, the empirical interest of the Scottish philosophers in the specific character of a given time, and of a place, its people and its culture. Having stumbled into this form in his first novel *Waverley*, Scott proceeded to systematically pursue his historicising mission in an extended series of novels, including his *Waverley* trilogy (1814–16), *Tales of my Landlord* (1816–32) and *Chronicles of the Canongate* (1827–28) and in four books of historical writing collectively entitled *Tales of a Grandfather (1828–30)*. No-one since Abbot Bower had attempted so monumentally to narrative the nation.

For all Scott's interest in balladry and folk tradition, his novels are an intensely literary and intellectual project, saturated with references to earlier books (Scottish, English and European) and driven by Enlightenment interests in philosophy, social affairs and economics. Moreover, the Scots language of the novels is confined to the direct speech of the characters and is given no role in the shaping of the author's narrative voice, which is expressed in formal English prose. The vivid Scots-speaking characters are often comic creations, animating the theatre of Scott's imagination, but they are permitted no share in the shaping of historical change. Such change is seen by Scott as an often regrettable but necessary process. The storytelling is designed to assist in understanding change but also in preserving a sense of continuity with the past and its values. The great achievement of Scott's novels was to provide a bridge with the past at a time of revolutionary change in Scottish life and his success is reflected in an immeasurable influence on nineteenth-century art, architecture, fiction, drama and popular culture in Scotland, Britain and beyond.

Heart of Midlothian (1818) is a good example of this process, dealing, as it does, with a sensitive period after the Union of the Parliaments, when the religious and political struggles of the previous generation are still a live memory and Jacobitism a present political reality. The depiction of Edinburgh's Porteous Riots in *Heart of Midlothian* is one of Scott's finest achievements as a novelist, capturing the mood of a city in which the sense of popular resentment and political grievance spills over into an act of potential revolution. Scott is sympathetic to the Scottish case and deft in his portrayal of the political context. However, beginning with the riots, he develops the conflict of the novel around a drama of personal moral decision – Jeannie Deans' refusal to lie in court to save Effie, her sister – and her consequent plea for a personal pardon for Effie from the Queen in London. Through *Heart of Midlothian*, Scott the Unionist vividly relives tensions within the Scotland/ England relationship at a critical period and creates a fiction which, in turn, became part of popular history. *Heart of Midlothian* provided one of Scottish theatre's most popular nineteenth-century plays, while places associated with the novel and Jeannie Deans in Edinburgh are part of the folk culture which no longer regards the story as fiction.

In effect, Scott's novels and the characters in them became part of the new popular traditions in a city- and town-based society but, as cultural artifacts, the novels are distanced from traditional society and the makers of oral narrative. This perception can, however, be qualified by an examination of Scott's *Tales of a Grandfather* which are built around the narrative device of the author telling his own grandson the story of Scotland. The emphasis here is on continuity as Scott draws directly on the Scottish chroniclers, historians and balladeers of previous generations, though within a new master narrative, leading to the Union of the English and Scottish Parliaments in 1707. This Union, Scott states at the outset, is the natural condition of the island of Britain and centuries of unnatural division had led to war and conflict. At the close of the *Tales*, Scott returns to this theme at length, ascribing the events leading to the Union to the guiding hand of Providence.

The clear implication of this narrative framing is that

Scotland should not have had a separate political identity or history in the first place and that these factors ended with the Union of 1707. Scottish history has, according to Scott, now ended – so why write about it? The reality is that Scott is moved and inspired by his narrative in the *Tales*, which reaches its finest passage in the accounts of the Jacobite Risings after 1707. Unlike Abbot Bower, Scott is unable to apply his master narrative with consistency and his main achievement is to perpetuate in a romanticised form the epic or tragic drama of Scottish nationhood which is deeply embedded in his sources.

Like other traditional historians influenced by the prestige of the Stewart monarchy, Scott skimps on the multiracial development of early Scotland and begins with Macbeth. Macbeth provides his first extended piece of storytelling, which is based on Hector Boece's account, replete with the witches and Banquo's ghost anomalously prophesying the Stewart line. Boece's account, which also informs Shakespeare's sources, is, in turn, based on a piece of early medieval history-making, *The Stewartis Oryginale*, which Andrew of Wyntoun ascribed to Barbour. Moving through the royal descendants of Malcolm Canmore and Queen Margaret, Scott's account of feudalism is a sympathetic one, but this feeling does not extend to Edward I of England's 'secret and unjust purpose' to lay claim to Scotland as his own. For Scott, as for Bower and the chroniclers, Alexander III's untimely death was a disaster and the trials of the nation had begun.

In presenting the full heroic saga of Wallace and Bruce, Scott appeals to the formula 'according to the old traditions of Scotland'. This accreditation leaves him free to redeploy and embroider material which is informed by his wide reading and his fondness for a good story, rather than by strict standards of historical authenticity. It is one of Scott's many paradoxes that his apparently historical work is much less critical in its approach than his sophisticated fictions. His account of John Comyn's murder by Bruce at Dumfries is a typical example of how the would-be historian slipped smoothly into storytelling mode:

They met in the church of the Minorites in that town, before the high altar. What passed betwixt them is not known with certainty; but they quarrelled, either concerning their mutual pretensions to the crown, or because Comyn refused to join Bruce in the proposed insurrection against the English; or, as many writers say, because Bruce charged Comyn with having betrayed to the English his purpose of rising up against King Edward. It is, however, certain that these two haughty barons came to high and abusive words, until at length Bruce who I told you was extremely passionate, forgot the sacred character of the place in which they stood and struck Comyn a blow with his dagger. Having done this rash deed he instantly ran out of the church and called for his horse. Two gentlemen of the country, Lindesay and Kirkpatrick, friends of Bruce were then in attendance on him. Seeing him pale, bloody and in much agitation, they eagerly inquired what was the matter.

'I doubt,' said Bruce, 'that I have slain the Red Comyn.'

'Do you leave such a matter in doubt?' said Kirkpatrick. 'I will make sicker!' – that is, I will make certain.

Accordingly he and his companion Lindesay rushed into the church and made the matter certain with a vengeance by dispatching the wounded Comyn with their daggers. His uncle, Sir Robert Comyn, was slain at the same time.[24]

In this case, Scott is encapsulating many previous versions in a brief, convincing narrative. In other instances, he draws on previously ungathered tales, such as the subsequently famous anecdote of Bruce and the spider, which, according to Scott, 'rests only on tradition in families of the name of Bruce' but 'is rendered probable by the manners of the time'.[25]

The hugely influential version of Mary Queen of Scots as tragic queen and martyr, which still holds sway in popular consciousness, owes more to Scott's *Tales of a Grandfather* than has often been acknowledged. Without concealing or denying Mary's faults and misjudgements, Scott consistently employs sympathy and pathos in his depiction of Mary, while steadily undermining any potential sympathy for the Lords of the Congregation in Scotland or for Elizabeth I in England – loyalty to Scotland's legitimate sovereign is always a virtue. Scott's account of the murder of David Rizzio, the queen's Italian courtier, by the Scottish nobility is a visually compelling portrait of a cultured sensitive ruler among violent barbarians:

> Queen Mary, like her father James V, was fond of laying aside the state of a sovereign and indulging in small private parties, quiet as she termed them and merry. On these occasions she admitted her favourite domestics to her table and Rizzio seems frequently to have had that honour. On the 9th of March 1566, six persons had partaken of supper in a small cabinet adjoining to the Queen's bedchamber, and having no entrance save through it. Rizzio was of the number. About seven in the evening, the gates of the palace were occupied by Morton, with a party of two hundred men; and a select band of the conspirators, headed by Darnley himself, came into the Queen's apartment by a secret stair-case. Darnley first entered the cabinet and stood for an instant in silence, gloomily eyeing his victim. Lord Ruthven followed in complete armour, looking pale and ghastly, as one scarcely recovered from long sickness. Others crowded in after them, till the little closet was full of armed men. While the Queen demanded the purpose of their coming, Rizzio who saw that his life was aimed at got behind her and clasped the folds of her gown, that the respect due to her person might protect him. The assassins threw down the table, and seized on the unfortunate object of their vengeance, while Darnley himself took hold of the Queen and forced Rizzio and her asunder. It was their intention, doubt-less, to have dragged Rizzio out of Mary's presence and to have killed him elsewhere; but their fierce impatience hurried them into instant murder. George Douglas, called the postulate of Arbroath, a natural brother of the Earl of Morton, set the example by snatching Darnley's dagger from his belt and striking Rizzio with it. He received many other blows. They dragged him through the bedroom and antechamber and despatched him at the head of the stair-

case, with no less than fifty-six wounds. Ruthven, after all was over, fatigued with his exertions, sate down in the Queen's presence and begging her pardon for the liberty called for a drink to refresh him, as if he had been doing the most harmless thing in the world.

The witnesses, the actors, and the scene of this cruel tragedy, render it one of the most extraordinary which history records. The cabinet and the bedroom still remain in the same condition in which they were at the time; and the floor near the head of the stair bears visible marks of the blood of the unhappy Rizzio. The Queen continued to beg his life with prayers and tears; but when she learned that he was dead she dried her tears. 'I will now,' she said, 'study revenge.'[26]

These particular splashes of blood could still be viewed at the Palace of Holyrood House in Edinburgh during my childhood and Rizzio's murder generated its own popular iconography of prints and film portrayals.[27]

As Mary's misfortunes deepen, Scott's designs on our sympathies increase and he strongly criticises the behaviour of both the Scottish and English governments towards the Queen in defeat, exile and imprisonment. By this point in the overall narrative, the richness of Scott's sources and his own imaginative involvement are lengthening the treatment relative to earlier periods, making Mary's death the emotional climax of the first series of *Tales*:

Mary received the melancholy intelligence with the utmost firmness. 'The soul,' she said, 'was undeserving of the joys of Heaven, which would shrink from the blow of an executioner.' She had not, she added, 'expected that her kinswoman would have consented to her death, but submitted not the less willingly to her fate.' She earnestly requested the assistance of a priest; but this favour which is granted to the worst criminals and upon which Catholics lay particular weight was cruelly refused. The Queen then wrote her last will and short and affectionate letters of farewell to her relations in France. She distributed among her attendants such valuables as had been left her and desired them to keep them for her sake. This occupied the evening before the day appointed for the fatal execution.

On the 8th February 1587, the Queen, still maintaining the same calm and undisturbed appearance which she had displayed at her pretended trial, was brought down to the great hall of the castle, where a scaffold was erected on which were placed a block and a chair, the whole being covered with black cloth. The Master of her Household, Sir Andrew Melville, was permitted to take a last leave of his mistress whom he had served long and faithfully. He burst into loud lamentations, bewailing her fate and deploring his own in being destined to carry such news to Scotland. 'Weep not, my good Melville,' said the Queen, 'but rather rejoice; for thou shalt this day see Mary Stewart relieved from all her sorrows.' She obtained permission with some difficulty that her maids should be allowed to attend her on the scaffold. It was objected to, that the extravagance of their grief might disturb the proceedings; she engaged for them that they would be silent.

When the Queen was seated in the fatal chair she heard the death warrants read by Beale, the clerk to the Privy Council, with an appearance of indifference; nor did she seem more attentive to the devotional exercises of the Dean of Peterborough in which as a Catholic she could not conscientiously join. She implored the mercy of Heaven, after the form prescribed by her own Church. She then prepared herself for execution, taking off such parts of her dress as might interfere with the deadly blow. The executioners offered their assistance, but she modestly refused it, saying she had neither been accustomed to undress before so many spectators nor to be served by such grooms of the chamber. She quietly chid her maids, who were unable to withhold their cries of lamentation, and reminded them that she had engaged for their silence. Last of all, Mary laid her head on the block, which the executioner severed from her body with two strokes of his axe. The headsman held it up in his hand, and the Dean of Peterborough cried out, 'So perish all Queen Elizabeth's enemies!' No voice, save that

of the Earl of Kent, could answer Amen: the rest were
choked with sobs and tears.[28]

Mary dies, Scott is telling us, as she lived – a true Queen
'eminent for beauty, for talent, and for accomplishments,
nor is there reason to doubt her natural goodness of heart
and courageous manliness of disposition'. Yet, a few chap-
ters earlier, Scott had been judiciously acknowledging that
Mary might have been implicated in the 'criminal' death of
her husband Darnley. Moreover, according to Scott's stated
master narrative, it is Mary's deposition and imprisonment
and the Scottish government's policy of non-involvement
which paved the way to the Union of the Scots and English
crowns in the person of her only son, the Protestant James
VI and I. But which aspect of Mary's death lives on in the
memory after reading the *Tales?* Again Scott has used his
sources – some of them eye witness accounts – to create a
simply constructed, coherent, cumulative narrative which
employs the strong visual imagery and the concentrated
dramatic dialogue of good oral narration.

Scott's account of the Wars of the Covenant in the *Tales,*
which he had already treated novelistically in *Old Mortality*
(1816), introduces a wealth of historical detail. He is not
emotionally sympathetic to the Covenanters or to Presbyter-
ianism in general but, after Montrose, the excesses of both
sides merit his disapproval. Given some of the accusations of
bias levelled against *Old Mortality,* Scott may have con-
strained his storytelling instincts in the interest of what he
perceived as balance. However, in these central sections of
the *Tales,* Scott takes increasing account of Highland affairs
and, from Killiecrankie through the massacre of Glencoe
and the 1715 Rising, the emotional temperature begins to
rise.

Scott's explicit thesis is again that the Union of the
Parliaments, however unequally conceived, was vital to
end war and division in Britain and to enable economic
development at home and imperial expansion abroad. So
the progress of history is validated by a rather vague appeal
to Providence. Consequently, the Jacobite Risings had to fail;

they were a backward step which could only provoke war and civil discord.

The problem, however, is that Scott intensely admires the courage and endeavour of the Jacobites, particularly in the rebellion of 1745:

Looking at the whole in a general point of view there can be no doubt that it presents a dazzling picture to the imagination, being a romance of real life equal in splendour and interest to any which could be devised by fiction. A primitive people, residing in a remote quarter of the empire and themselves but a small portion of the Scottish Highlanders, fearlessly attempted to place the British Crown on the head of the last scion of those ancient kings, whose descent was traced to their own mountains. This gigantic task they undertook in favour of a youth of twenty-five, who landed on their shore without support of any kind, and threw himself on their generosity – they assembled an army on his behalf – their speech, their tactics, their arms, were alike unknown to their countrymen and to the English; holding themselves free from the obligations imposed by common law or positive statute, they were yet governed by rules of their own, derived from a general sense of honour, extending from the chief to the lowest of his tribe. With men unaccustomed to arms, the amount of the most efficient part of which never exceeded 2000, they defeated two disciplined armies commanded by officers of experience and reputation, penetrated deep into England, approached within a hundred miles of the capital and made the crown tremble on the king's head; retreated with the like success, when they appeared on the point of being intercepted between three hostile armies; checked effectually the attack of a superior body detached in pursuit of them; reached the North in safety and were only suppressed by a concurrence of disadvantages which it was impossible for human nature to surmount. All this has much that is splendid to the imagination, nor is it possible to regard without admiration the little band of determined men by whom such actions were achieved, or the interesting young Prince by whom their

energies were directed. It is therefore natural that the civil
strife of 1745 should have been long the chosen theme of the
poet, the musician, and the novelist, and each has in turn
found it possessed of an interest highly suitable to his
purpose.[29]

Scott's admiration is directed towards the 'primitive'
values of honour and loyalty which he perceives as inherent
to clan society and motivational for the Jacobite cause.
Human will and courage can move events and challenge
progress and Providence, as Scott underlines in his account
of how Prince Charles lands in the Western Highlands and
personally sets the revolt in motion:

This memorable landing in Moidart took place on the 25th
July, 1745. The place where Charles was lodged was remarkably well situated for concealment and for communication
with friendly clans, both in the islands and on the mainland
without whose countenance and concurrence it was impossible that his enterprise could succeed.

Cameron of Lochiel had an early summons from the
Prince and waited on him as soon as he received it. He
came fully convinced of the utter madness of the undertaking and determined, as he thought, to counsel the
Adventurer to return to France and wait a more favourable
opportunity.

'If such is your purpose, Donald,' said Cameron of Fassiefern to his brother of Lochiel, 'write to the Prince your
opinion; but do not trust yourself within the fascination of
his presence. I know you better than you know yourself and
you will be unable to refuse compliance.'

Fassiefern prophesied truly. While the Prince confined
himself to argument Lochiel remained firm and answered
all his reasoning. At length Charles, finding it impossible to
subdue the chief's judgment, made a powerful appeal to his
feelings.

'I have come hither,' he said, 'with my mind unalterably
made up, to reclaim my rights or to perish. Be the issue what
will, I am determined to display my standard and take the

field with such as may join it. Lochiel, whom my father esteemed the best friend of our family, may remain at home and learn his Prince's fate from the newspapers.'

'Not so,' replied the chief, much affected, 'if you are resolved on this rash undertaking I will go with you and so shall every one over whom I have influence.'

Thus was Lochiel's sagacity overpowered by his sense of what he esteemed higher honour and loyalty which induced him to front the prospect of ruin with a disinterested devotion, not unworthy of the best days of chivalry. His decision was the signal for the commencement of the Rebellion; for it was generally understood at the time that there was not a chief in the Highlands who would have risen, if Lochiel had maintained his pacific purpose.[30]

The success of the rebellion is remarkable but the ultimate consequences are tragic and brutal for its supporters and for Highland society in general. Scott spares no detail of the victor's cruelty, yet, according to the 'sound rules of reason', the defeat was necessary. Out of this tension between different aspects of his Enlightenment inheritance, Scott produced his fiction and gave the nation a vivid, though self-divided, vision of its past. The emphasis here is on the past since, for Scott, the rebellion of 1745 is the end of his narrative:

Neither has any thing occurred in Scotland at large to furnish matter for the continuation of these narratives. She has, since 1746, regularly felt her share in the elevation or abasement of the rest of the empire. The civil war, a cruelly severe yet a most effectual remedy, had destroyed the seeds of disunion which existed in the bosom of Scotland; her commerce gradually increased and, though checked for a time by the American war, revived after the peace of of 1780 with a brilliancy of success hitherto unexampled. The useful arts, agriculture, navigation and all the aids which natural philosophy affords to industry, came in the train of commerce. The shocks which the country has sustained since the peace of 1815 have arisen out of causes general to the imperial kingdoms and not peculiar to Scotland. It may be added also that she has not borne more than her own share of the burden and may look forward with confidence to be relieved from it as early as any of the sister kingdoms.[31]

Scottish history is now British history and, as Scott's last sentence makes clear, Scottish and, in particular, Highland valour has been redirected towards defeating the French and building the British Empire. The result was a curiously bifocal view of Scotland in which the national past was to be treasured with heart and imagination but the national present and future must be sacrificed to 'the sound rule of reason' and the logic of economic progress.

As already indicated, Scott focused the dominant cultural view in Scotland for more than a century but his was not the only reading of the Scottish past. In a fine study, *The Rise of the Historical Novel* (1989), John MacQueen places Scott alongside two other important historical novelists, John Galt and James Hogg.[32] Collectively, these three writers represent a remarkable contribution by one small nation to the making of the historical novel but their collective contribution to understanding Scotland's story at a time of revolutionary change is invaluable. Despite, or perhaps because of, the rapidity of change, Scottish writers brought their Enlightenment understanding of society and a rich inheritance of literature and oral tradition to bear on the transformation of Scotland in the context of the American War of Independence, the French Revolution, the Napoleonic Wars, the Industrial Revolution and the agitation for political reform. There is a common desire to give a human account of the changes and to make some sense of what Scots had experienced and were still experiencing.

It is significant that, while Scott sees the Forty-five as the culmination of Scottish history, John Galt barely mentions it. His focus is on the shaping of Scottish society and culture from the time of the Reformation by the economic, political and religious outworkings of Protestantism. Like Scott, Galt views this process as a religious providence but the Ayrshire novelist means this in the much more definite sense of

Calvinist necessity. In his novel of Covenanting times *Ringan Gilhaize* (1823), Galt uses two interwoven first person narratives to trace the struggle and gradual progress of Protestant society from the Reformation to the Presbyterian settlement of 1690. This national historical development underlies the more recent social and economic changes, minutely recorded in the first person testimony of the Reverend Balwhidder in *Annals of the Parish* (1821). Despite his fondness for first person narration, Galt is a literary artist little influenced by oral form or method. He is antipathetic to Scott's emotional identification with certain aspects of the past and employs irony in both subtle and direct ways to distance the reader from his narrator's viewpoint.

Although Galt is both a humane and humorous artist, his presentation of Scotland has always been too rigorous and uncomfortably honest to appeal to a majority audience. However, his emphasis on Protestantism and on the Covenanting Wars as the decisive struggle for a modern Scotland has had enthusiastic advocates among historians since the seventeenth-century church historian, David Calderwood, took up his pen.[33] In addition, the popular traditions and folklore of the Covenanters still has its devotees in Ayrshire, Dumfriesshire and the Borders, where remote landscapes are memorialised by the tragic persecutions of this period.

The third writer in MacQueen's triumvirate, James Hogg, was severely undervalued until the twentieth century, when the French novelist André Gide championed his *Private Memoirs and Confessions of a Justified Sinner* (1824) as a modern literary masterpiece. Like Galt and Scott, Hogg's narrative art reaches back through poetry and fiction into Scotland's medieval and more recent past. Hogg's most popular poetic work, *The Queen's Wake* (1813), uses the device of minstrels competing over three nights at the court of Queen Mary to be acclaimed the champion of narrative verse. In *The Three Perils of Man: War, Women and Witchcraft* (1822) Hogg produces a compendious epic based on Borders tradition. Unified by a Romance storyline, the novel contains tales within the tales and employs a range of fantasy, mock epic and satiric modes in a rumbustious and sparkling tribute to the oral tale tellers. Hogg's *Brownie of Bodsbeck* (1818) records the harsh 'killing times' of the Covenanting persecution as a riposte to Scott's title *Old Mortality*. His work is alive with a rich diversity of oral voices and dialect.

Hogg is acutely aware of social and economic change and of the erosion of the older communal values. He is also, despite the caricature of a pastoral boor generated by Edinburgh's literary fraternity, fully aware of the Enlightenment analysis of the logic and necessity of such change. But Hogg's originality in his short stories and novels is to challenge this analysis and to place the supernatural and spiritual beliefs of traditional culture on an equal footing with the secularising Enlightenment. Within his often complex literary artefacts, Hogg uses traditional styles of storytelling and the perceptions of traditional culture as a form of truth-to-experience, without which the strangeness of human personal and social psychology is inexplicable. The social forces of economic progress may be ineluctable but that does not make the Enlightenment view of humankind necessarily true or ultimately satisfying. The message of Hogg's masterly *Memoirs and Confessions* seems to be that overdependence on rationality may divide the personality against itself and deprive people of the ability to convey to themselves and others a unity of lived experience. The motif of the double or doppelgänger returns in modern Scottish literature, notably in Stevenson's *The Strange Case of Dr Jekyll and Mr Hyde* (1886) and in the humanistic psychology of R. D. Laing's *The Divided Self* (1959).[34]

Hogg found the imaginative resources of meaning and expression to create his independent storytelling art in the balladry and folk tale amongst which he had been reared in his Borders childhood. Being essentially an autodidact, Hogg, the shepherd, had experienced a deeply rooted way of life before he absorbed and utilised literary and intellectual thinking as Hogg, the writer. This is the source of both the strangeness and the originality of his art and is part of the reason why it was so marginalised in Scotland until the late twentieth century. During his own lifetime,

Hogg's fiction was severely criticised and the closer he came in period to the contemporary world, the more hostile the attacks became. Pleasing neither the godly, the intellectual nor the respectable, it must have taken courage and integrity for Hogg to continue stubbornly practising his art in his own way. Even Hogg's two-volume collection of authentic Jacobite songs and verse was criticised for lacking the true Romantic spirit of Jacobitism! Only now, with the gradual republication of Hogg's corpus in the form originally intended by its author, are we coming to see Hogg's narrative art as an ambitious whole capable of challenging Scott's cultural hegemony.

Scott's storytelling provided the majority, or at least dominant, cultural view in Scotland for at least a century, while Galt is the more rigorous and sophisticated exponent of religion and the rise of capitalism. But it is Hogg, the Ettrick Shepherd, who reaches furthest back into Scotland's cultural past and points forward to a period in which the limitations of scientific progress are widely canvassed and oral traditions are once again highly valued. Perhaps Hogg's best time is still to come.

Notes

1. See Burns *Poems and Songs* edited by Kinsley, James (1971), Oxford: Oxford University Press, pp. 29–31.
2. The closeness of the brothers Chambers and their influence on each other is well-represented by the *Memoir of William and Robert Chambers* (1883), Edinburgh: W. & R. Chambers, which combines memoir and autobiography by both.
3. See Chambers, Robert (1825), *Illustrations of the Author of Waverley*, Edinburgh: W. & R. Chambers; *Domestic Annals of Scotland* Vol. 1 (1859) Edinburgh: W. & R. Chambers; and Vols 2 and 3 (1874), Edinburgh: W. & R. Chambers; *History of the Rebellion of 1745–6* (1869), Edinburgh: W. & R. Chambers; *The Life and Works of Robert Burns* (1852–4), Edinburgh: W. & R. Chambers. Robert Chambers also published anonymously his remarkable theory of evolution *Vestiges of the Natural History of Creation* (1843–46) Edinburgh: W & R Chambers.
4. Chambers, Robert [1826] (1841) *The Popular Rhymes of Scotland*, Edinburgh: W. & R. Chambers, p. v–vi.

5. Ibid. p. vi.
6. Quoted in Glen, Duncan (1995), *A Nation in a Parish*, Edinburgh: Akros Publications, p. 152.
7. Quoted in Ibid. p. 153.
8. Ibid., p. 153.
9. See Leonard, Tom (ed.) *Radical Renfrew* (1990), Edinburgh: Polygon, pp. 8–32. For a full account of Wilson's remarkable career see Cantwell, Robert (1961), *Alexander Wilson: Naturalist and Pioneer*, New York and Philadelphia: J. B. Lippencott Company.
10. See *Radical Renfrew*, passim.
11. Quoted in Buchan, Norman 'Folk and Protest' in Cowan, Edward J. (ed.) (1980), *The People's Past: Scottish Folk Scottish History*, Edinburgh: Polygon, p. 170.
12. Quoted in Logue, Kenneth, 'Eighteenth Century Popular Protest' in *The People's Past: Scottish Folk, Scottish History*.
13. Quoted in Hunter, James (1999), *Last of the Free: A Millennial History of the Highlands and Islands of Scotland*, Edinburgh: Mainstream Publishing, p. 268.
14. Quoted in Ibid. p. 269.
15. Quoted in Ibid. p. 269.
16. Quoted in Ibid. p. 301.
17. Ibid. p. 301.
18. See Donaldson, William (1986), *Popular Literature in Victorian Scotland*, Aberdeen: Aberdeen University Press; and Donaldson, William (ed.) (1989), *The Language of the People*, Aberdeen: Aberdeen University Press.
19. *The Language of the People*, p. 50.
20. *Popular Literature in Victorian Scotland*, p. 76.
21. Ibid. pp. 76–7.
22. Ibid. pp. 120–1.
23. Ibid. pp. 122–3.
24. Scott, Sir Walter (1847), *Tales of a Grandfather*, Vol. 1, Edinburgh: Robert Cadell, pp. 50–1.
25. Ibid. p. 27.
26. Ibid. pp. 249–50.
27. Those who think Scott's visual influence did not continue into the twentieth century should view John Ford's *Mary of Scotland* (1936) which adds the power of Hollywood to the Victorian prints and the earlier stage melodramas and silent films.
28. *Tales of a Grandfather*, Vol. 1, pp. 288–9.
29. *Tales of a Grandfather*, Vol. 3, pp. 326–7.

30. Ibid. pp. 161–2.
31. Ibid. p. 344.
32. See, MacQueen John (1989), *The Rise of the Historical Novel*, Edinburgh: Scottish Academic Press, passim.
33. See Calderwood, David (1842–9), *The History of the Kirk of Scotland*, 8 Vols edited by Thomson, T., Edinburgh: The Woodrow Society.
34. See Laing, R. D. (1959), *The Divided Self*, London: Tavistock Publications; and Laing, R. D. (1985), *Wisdom, Madness and Folly* introduced by Beveridge, Craig and Turnbull, Ronald, Edinburgh: Canongate Classics.

Twentieth-Century Voices

───────◆───────

At the start of the third millennium, we can talk about the twentieth century as a whole and measure the social and political changes of the last one hundred years. From the perspective of a newly devolved Scotland with its first democratic parliament, these have been considerable. It is much harder to define the nature of the century's cultural changes. The Scottish Renaissance movement can be seen, in one aspect, as an attempt to reconnect with older narratives and this is evident in poetry, fiction, theatre and film. However, the contexts have changed and the meaning of older symbols and patterns cannot be presumed in an era when artists have grappled with radical discontinuity. The twentieth century also brought a 'rediscovery' of living oral traditions in the lingering Hebridean Gaeltacht and amongst the Scottish Travellers. How is the significance of these and other oral voices to be measured within the wider cultural framework?

In 1900, the sense of Scottishness which was described in the last chapter remained strong and influential on popular culture, though the rural imagery surrounding it had become removed from the reality and inclined towards kailyard nostalgia. In comparison, identification with the British Empire was at its peak and the popular militarism surrounding the imperial cause was an important aspect of Scottish life. Scottish regiments had played a numerically disproportionate role in the British Army since the late eighteenth century and, since the Napoleonic Wars, a mythology and tradition of martial valour had grown up around their often humdrum service. Heroic images of the capture of a French standard at Waterloo by Ensign Ewart of the Royal Scots

Greys; the 'thin red line' of the 93rd (Highland) Regiment at Balaclava; and the bayonet charge at Tel-el-Kebir in the Egyptian campaign of 1882, sustained the myth and encouraged recruitment.[1] Scott had laid the foundations but, by the late nineteenth century, the imperial venture commanded majority popular support in Scotland, though political opinion was still divided on individual empire-building ventures.

Imperialism was closely connected in the public imagination with war but explorers and missionaries were also popular figures. Again Scotland contributed disproportionately, with missionaries and explorers being exemplified in the career of David Livingstone. Not only was Livingstone an example of the 'lad o pairts' who made good despite poverty and humble origins, but his pioneering travels, missionary commitment and his opposition to slavery, made him a nineteenth-century Scottish Protestant hero on a par with John Knox.[2] Stories of missionaries and explorers were circulated in book form, in prints and pamphlets, through sermons and lectures and by the formidable machinery of the popular press.

The role of missionaries in nineteenth century Scottish culture reflects the organisational and numerical strength of the mainstream Christian denominations in Scottish society and the accelerating expansion of institutional religion in Scotland from the 1830s. Twentieth-century ecclesiastical apologists lamented the relative decline of institutional religion as if the nineteenth-century boom represented a Scottish norm. This is far from the truth since, although Christianity played a vital spiritual, social and political role in national life, active religious vocation was a strictly minority pursuit in Scotland until the nineteenth century. In both the Reformation and Covenanting periods, social and religious change were achieved by political alliances between effectively secular leaders and an active religious minority. Church allegiance for the majority was more of a social concern as opposed to a metaphysical belief, which was presumed, or a spiritual experience which was no more frequent then than now.

However, the great social and economic dislocations of the early nineteenth century brought in their train a new style of church organisation and a steady growth in personal religious commitment. For many, in a dramatically changed urban environment, the churches provided an essential social framework as well as spiritual support.[3] Religion developed its own popular culture with shared stories and iconography – Protestant and later Catholic and Episcopalian. Unfortunately, church leaders, with distinguished exceptions, were often more intent on securing allegiance to their institution than ensuring the relevance of their mission to the social and psychological conditions of the majority Scottish population.[4] The energy of organised religion and its balance of strengths and weaknesses are encapsulated in the 1843 Disruption of the Church of Scotland and in the subsequent rapid growth of the Free Church as a separate denomination. At the centre of that ecclesiastical revolution was another towering nineteenth-century hero, Thomas Chalmers, a figure comparable in his day to Knox and Livingstone, but now all but forgotten outwith church history.

The long nineteenth century, which was characterised by a historically orientated Scottish culture, imperialism and religion, came to a catastrophic end between 1914 and 1918. Apart from the loss of life (148,000 Scots were killed on active service) and the legacy of physical and psychological injury, religious and political certainties foundered in the Flanders mud. What had victory and its appalling price really achieved? Could it any longer be said that *dulce et decorum est pro patria mori*? Slowly but surely Britishness came under question and the 1920s brought the first minority stirrings of Scottish nationalism. During the same twenties, the National War Memorial was taking shape in Edinburgh Castle. This ordered masterwork by Robert Lorimer is celebrated for its dignity and the integrated way in which the art works and the building complement each other. But there is a gap between these dignities in stone and bronze and the brutal realities of human beings, harnessed to the destructive and degrading power of modern industrial war machines. As the Memorial was completed in 1929, the seeds of Nazism had already been sown by the European powers in the punitive peace at Versailles. Amongst these contradictions a Scottish cultural renaissance began, spearheaded by the volcanic talent of the poet Hugh MacDiarmid.

MacDiarmid's foundational work is an epic soliloquy, *A Drunk Man Looks at the Thistle* (1926), which reflects on the nature of Scottishness and appeals to a worldwide range of philosophical, political and literary sources. The poetry is often discursive but reaches towards symbolism and shifts, in sections, to the formal self-sufficient qualities of the lyric. In this sense, *A Drunk Man* is a modernist work stressing radical discontinuities with past forms and narratives, as well as the revolutionary nature of the present: all the energy and dislocation of the modern consciousness is soliloquised. Yet, in his hunger for symbolism, MacDiarmid also appeals to underlying continuities. The drunk man lying contemplating a thistle is on his way home from the pub to his wife Jean. He experiences the same pattern of descent into and ascent from a mystical or supernatural experience, as Tam o' Shanter suffered on his way home to his wife Kate. Will the outcome of this adventure be any more positive? Could it involve the retrieval of poetic, philosophic and even political wisdom of the kind ascribed to Thomas the Rhymer in his journey to the otherside of imagination and spiritual energy? MacDiarmid's protagonist is in this tradition.

To engage with older narratives and symbols, while radically questioning and perhaps renewing their vitality, is characteristic of Scottish writers in the twentieth century. As well as MacDiarmid, these included Edwin Muir, Neil Gunn, Sorley Maclean, Lewis Grassic Gibbon and Naomi Mitchison, to name only a few. Muir's often anthologised poem 'Scotland 1941' for example, seeks living symbols amongst the nation's historical narrative:

> We were a family, a tribe, a people,
> Wallace and Bruce guard now a painted field,

And all may read the folio of our fable,
Peruse the sword, the sceptre and the shield.
A simple sky roofed in that rustic day,
The busy corn-fields and the haunted holms,
The green path winding up the ferny brae.
But Knox and Melville clapped their preaching palms
And huddled all the harvest gold away,
Hoodicrow Peden in the blighted corn
Hacked with his rusty beak the starving haulms,
Out of that desolation we were born.
Courage beyond the point and obdurate pride
Gave us a nation, robbed us of a nation.
Defiance absolute and myriad-eyed
That could not pluck the palm plucked our damnation.
We with such courage and the bitter wit
To fell the ancient oak of loyalty,
And strip the peopled hill and the altar bare,
And crush the poet with an iron text,
How could we read our souls and learn to be?
If we could raise those bones so brave and wrong,
Revive our ancient body, part by part.
We'd touch to pity the annalist's iron tongue
And gather a nation in our sorrowful heart.[5]

The historical accuracy of this account of Scottish culture
has often been challenged: was Protestantism really a cultural blight or did it foster education and literacy?[6] But the
search for a source on which to base renewal of the national
narrative is a constant ground.

In seeking to renew a continuity which seemed to have
been broken by history, some writers turned to the Enlightenment inheritance of anthropological and historicist thinking, exemplified in the work of Scots such as James Frazer
and William Robertson Smith. Lewis Grassic Gibbon's trilogy, *A Scots Quair* (1932–34), traces the descent of human
culture from a golden age, leading to severance of the
connection between land and people by war and economic
oppression. Out of this crux, Gibbon tries to fashion a new
collective socialist narrative of conflict and potential libera-

tion. Naomi Mitchison draws more directly on Frazer's
Golden Bough (1890–1915) in her *The Corn King and the
Spring Queen* (1931) for a background of collective symbolism taken from the natural world. In her *The Bull Calves*
(1947), which is a modern commentary on Scott and Stevenson's historical fiction written in the aftermath of World
War II, she also turns to socialism and a Jungian analysis of
psychological integration to create a specifically Scottish
psychodrama of renewal.

Other authors wrote directly from the historical experience of their community, with little sense of interpretative
mediation since the narrative itself provides its own symbolism and challenge. This is particularly true of Gaelic writers
such as Sorley Maclean whose *Hallaig* is the keynote
twentieth-century poem in Gaelic:

'Time, the deer, is in the wood of Hallaig'
The window is nailed and boarded
through which I saw the West
and my love is at the Burn of Hallaig,
a birch tree, and she has always been

between Inver and Milk Hollow,
here and there about Baile-chuirn
she is a birch, a hazel,
a straight, slender young rowan.

In Screapadal of my people
where Norman and Big Hector were,
their daughter and their sons are a wood
going up beside the stream.

Proud tonight the pine cocks
crowing on the top of Cnoc an Ra,
straight their backs in the moonlight –
they are not the wood I love.

I will wait for the birch wood
until it comes up by the cairn,

until the whole ridge from Beinn na Lice
will be under its shade.

If it does not, I will go down to Hallaig,
to the Sabbath of the dead,
where the people are frequenting,
every single generation gone.

They are still in Hallaig
MacLeans and MacLeods,
All who were there in the time of MacGille Chaluim:
the dead have been seen alive.

The men lying on the green
at the end of every house that was,
the girls a wood of birches,
straight their backs, bent their heads.

Between the Leac and Fearns
the road is under mild moss
and the girls in silent bands
go to Clachan as in the beginning,

and return from Clachan
from Suisnish and the land of the living;
each one young and light stepping,
without the hearbreak of the tale.

'Tha tim, am fiadh, an coille Hallaig'
Tha bùird is tàirnean air an uinneig
troimh'm faca mi an Aird an Iar
's tha mo ghaol aig Allt Hallaig
'na craiobh bheithe,'s bha i riamh

eadar an t-Inbhir's Poll a'Bhainne,
thall's a bhos mu Bhaile-Chùirn:
tha i 'na beithe, 'na calltuinn,
'na caorunn dhìeach sheang ùir.

127

Ann an Screapadal mo chinnidh
far robh Tarmad's Eachunn Mòr,
tha'n nigheanan's am mic'nan coille
ag gabhail suas ri taobh an lóin.

Uaibhreach a nochd na coilich ghuithais
ag gairm air mullach Cnoc an Rà,
dìreach an druim ris a'ghealaich –
chan iadsan coille mo ghràidh.

Fuirichidh me ris a'bheithe
gus an tig i mach an Càrn,
gus am bi am bearadh uile
o Bheinn na Lice f' a sgàil.

Mura tig's ann theàrnas mi a Hallaig
a dh'ionnsaigh sàbaid nam marbh,
far a bheil an sluagh a'tathaich,
garch aon ghinealach a dh'fhalbh.

Tha iad fhathast ann a Hallaig
Clann Ghill-Eain's Clann MhicLeòid,
na bh'ann ri linn Mhic Ghille-Chaluim:
chunnacas na mairbh beo.

Na fir'nan laighe air an lianaig
aig ceann gach taighe a bh'ann,
na h-igheanan'nan coille bheithe,
dìreach an druim, crom an ceann.

Eadar an Leac is na Fearnaibh
tha'n rathad mòr fo chòinnich chiùin,
s na h-igheanan'nam badan sàmhach
a'dol a Chlachan mar o thùs

agus a'tilleadh as a'Chlachan,
á Suidhisnis's á tir nam beò;
a chuile té òg uallach
gun bhristeadh cridhe an sgeòil.[7]

The poem continues until it achieves a symbolic and emotional resolution in the image of the deer of time, stricken by the hunter's gun. But the overwhelming sense is that the landscape itself has become the bearer of a historical narrative and of an experience which remains powerfully eloquent.

In general, twentieth-century writers echoed the concerns with landscape, myth, history, social change and moral sense which characterised story makers in Scotland during previous centuries, though they did so in a diverse and eclectic range of forms and linguistic styles. In the past, this diversity of form and method misled many critics into believing that Scotland did not have a distinctive modern literary tradition, but recent commentators, such as Cairns Craig, have corrected this misconception by tracing these characteristic concerns across genres and relating them to the Scottish cultural background.[8] Cairns Craig's case is greatly strengthened if the same thematic comparisons are extended into drama and film.

The interaction between myth and literature, which is characteristic of the twentieth-century Scottish poetry and fiction, is also evident in twentieth-century Scottish drama. J. M. Barrie's theatrical oeuvre is based on a highly conscious and crafted manipulation of myth and its meanings, not least in *Peter Pan* (1904), and *Mary Rose* (1920) where Highland legend and landscape are used to evoke the pathos and tragedy of lost time and lost experience. James Bridie, another of Scotland's leading twentieth-century playwrights, constantly strove to juxtapose a mythic underlay with a comedy or tragicomedy of manners. In *The Forrigan Reel* (1944), there is an explicit comic exploration of Highland myth and legend; in the *Baikie Charivari* (1952), middle class west coast mores are set against the masks and grotesques of *commedia dell' arte*; in *The Queen's Comedy* (1950), the aftermath of World War II is explored through a reworking of Greek myth that questions religious faith in the light of human suffering. In *Tobias and the Angel* (1930) and *Susannah and the Elders* (1937), Bridie cleverly deploys Jewish stories from the Apocrypha to challenge and explore the protestant consciousness and conscience of Scotland's middle classes.

Amongst later dramatists, Rona Munro uses the mythology of landscape, and in particular of Bennachie, to give psychological depth and intensity to her counterpointed tale of the struggles of a nineteenth-century actress-manager in *The Maiden Stone* (1995). Stephen Greenhorn's *Passing Places* (1997) is subtitled 'a road movie for the stage' and combines the classic filmic form with an archetypal Scottish journey from the industrialised central belt to the supposed wilderness of the Highlands. 'In a Scottish road movie,' commented the Traverse Theatre's Director, Philip Howard, 'the Going West of the American Dream is, of course, replaced by a Going North. The "surfing paradise" of Thurso becomes a new *ultima Thule.*'[9] Bridie and Barrie's influence on later Scottish theatre has been obscured because the social mores reflected in their work were so rapidly overtaken.

In all of these cases, myth is treated as a still active source of meaning and value through which a questioning and troublesome modernity can be reflected. A further group of twentieth-century Scottish plays are set at key ritual or transitional moments in Scottish life, such as a funeral or at New Year. The dramatic setting identifies with an older tradition of communal identity and the plays' themes of conflict are heightened by a resonance of the wider existential struggles between life and death, light and darkness, winter and spring or good and evil. Among these plays, Joe Corrie's *In Time of Strife* (1929) is set in the Fife mining community during the strike of 1926; Ena Lamont Stewart's *Men Should Weep* [1947] (1982) is set in a Glasgow working class community in the 1930s; while Tony Roper's hugely popular *The Steamie* (1987) is set in the communal washhouse in Glasgow on a 1950s Hogmanay. Sidney Goodsir Smith's (as yet unperformed) Rabelaisian epic drama *Colicky Meg* explores the ritual and mythology of Hogmanay itself.

Moving pictures on film and video may come to be seen as the characteristic art form of the twentieth century but Scottish film makers and makers of Scottish films – not always the same thing – have remained very close to the central storytelling concerns which have been identified in oral tradition and literature.[10] Similar mythic territories are deployed in a variety of genres. In the rural idyll or comedy, Scottish film has often used the visual power of landscape to portray an ideal unity of land and community against which the false sophistication or misconceived values of modernity are contrasted. Notable examples include Alexander Mackendrick's *Whisky Galore* (1948), John Eldridge's *Laxdale Hall* (1952) and Bill Forsyth's *Local Hero* (1983). The emotionally opposite genre of elegy or lament has been used by film to explore the same myth in Michael Powell's *The Edge of the World* (1937) and Bill Bryden's television film *Ill Fares the Land* (1982) which both feature the remote Hebridean isle of St Kilda and its evacuation. What were the implications for twentieth-century civilisation if, after so many centuries, life on these 'lost paradises' had become unsustainable?

The interest of filmmakers in a presumed communal innocence and its potential or actual violation is also evident in a series of films based on the perspective of childhood. This same focus is central to the work of Scottish novelists, such as Robin Jenkins and Jessie Kesson, whose first person narratives interweave childhood perceptions with adult experience. It is also integral to the popular genre of autobiographical memoir, both as a fictional form in prose and drama and as a type of biography. Autobiographical memoirs based on the interaction of innocence and experience include Betsy Whyte's *The Yellow on the Broom* (1979), the rural story of a young Scottish Traveller, and Ralph Glasser's *Growing up in the Gorbals* 1986), the urban story of a young Glaswegian. In film form, the first example of childhood perspective is Philip Leacock's *The Kidnappers* (1953) based on Neil Paterson's screenplay which Paterson adapted from his own novella. But it was the Scottish director, Bill Douglas who took this form to a new level of artistic intensity in his autobiographical trilogy, in particular with his first two films, *My Childhood* (1972) and *My Ain Folk* (1973).[11] The television adaptation of Jessie Kesson's *White Bird Passes* was another child's eye view, as was Ian Seller's film, *Venus Peter* (1989), based on a book by Christopher Rush.

In the late nineties, Lynne Ramsay's *Ratcatcher* (1999) combined the perspective of childhood with the visual impact of a post-industrial urban wasteland. The desolation of this film is a late twentieth-century commentary on the depiction in Scottish literature, film and theatre of a depressed urban community. Victimised by distant and uncontrollable economic forces, and severely pressurised by poverty and social injustice, the community strives heroically to sustain its identity and/or succumb to the violent mores and spiritual despair of the urban environment. Films in this succession include David MacKane's *The Gorbals Story* (1950); John Mackenzie and Peter McDougall's *Just Another Saturday* (1975); the same creative team's *A Sense of Freedom* (1981) which is based on the autobiography of gangster-turned-artist Jimmy Boyle; John Hodge's and Danny Boyle's film adaptation of Irvine Welsh's *Trainspotting* (1996); and Ken Loach's *My Name is Joe* (1998). Black humour, violence and phantasmagoric urban backgrounds abound in reaction to a destructive twentieth-century rhythm, alternating between decaying ghettos and the clearances of the population to new housing schemes, 'dear green places' bereft of human infrastructure. The nineteenth-century experience lived on in modern form, while memories of earlier clearances strengthened rather than diminished.

In most of these examples, film and theatre makers have harnessed the symbolic and emotional force of collective mythologies to some form of social or moral analysis, but there is also a temptation to exploit the appeal. This tension is evident in twentieth-century film makers' use of Scottish history as a source of narrative myth and legend. Mel Gibson's *Braveheart* (1995), Scottish film's biggest ever Hollywood success since *Brigadoon* (1954), is unashamed in its portrayal of the barbarian but freedom-loving warrior Celts, at one with the land but driven to desperation by cruel feudal oppressors. Perhaps its most enduring legacy is the adoption by football fans worldwide of Gibson's mask-like face-painting technique, based on a dream or vision of Blind Hary's *Wallace* in which the Virgin Mary paints a Saltire on Wallace's face.[12] Scottish politicians were also suspiciously

eager to identify with this popular travesty of Scottish culture
and politics, set in a period when the historical William
Wallace actually sought to defend the legacy of two centuries
of civilised kingship. By contrast, in her popular stage play
Mary Queen of Scots Got Her Head Chopped Off (1987), Liz
Lochhead deconstructs the romantic myth of the tragic
queen in a robust and subversive piece of narrative theatre
driven by the raucous and balladic Scots voice of Corbie who
embodies an ironic and deflating alternative oral tradition.
Ronald Neame's *Tunes of Glory* (1960), based on a novel and
screenplay by James Kennaway, demonstrates that film can
also anatomise mythologies and stereotypes. Set in Stirling
Castle, *Tunes of Glory* lays bare the human cost of the military
code of 'honour' and puts the background of Scotland's
British history – army, Empire and the class system – under a
remorseless lens.

History continued to provide Scottish twentieth-century
writers with a rich source book of imagined worlds. While
R. L. Stevenson, John Buchan and Neil Munro explored the
psychological and cultural contrasts embedded in historical
narratives, Nigel Tranter literally retrod the landscape,
personalities and events of Scottish history in a stream of
novels and guide books. Yet these historic territories were
constantly being expanded by new perspectives on Scotland's multi-faceted history. Building on the industrious
achievement of nineteenth-century conservers and editors,
twentieth-century Scottish historiography spawned a wealth
of research and specialist studies. The geographical and
cultural territory known as Scotland has been revealed as a
multi-racial, regionally diverse, internationally contextua-
lised society. Each historiographical landmark such as the
four volume *Edinburgh History of Scotland* (1965–74) is built
on innumerable microcosmic researches into this mutli-
layered phenomenon. The publication of T. C. Smout's
History of the Scottish People 1560–1830 in 1969 marked a shift
of emphasis to accounting for the experience of Scotland's
socially and geographically diverse population in the modern centuries. This was succeeded in 1986 by his *A Century of
the Scottish People 1830–1950* which utilised oral sources to

view the national experience from new persepctives. Towards the end of the twentieth century, there was a revival in
the genre of one-volume narrative history with Michael
Lynch's *Scotland, A New History* (1991) and T. M. Devine's
The Scottish Nation 1700–2000 (1999) reaching for synthesis.
Following the re-establishment of the Scottish Parliament in
1999, the thesis that Scotland's complex nationhood had
continued to develop beyond 1707 seemed to be vindicated.
The interaction between past history and present understanding was set to become an even more fertile and intriguing source for storytellers and storymakers in different
media.

For example, the Norse theme in Scottish history and
culture had been marginalised in previous centuries by the
need to bolster the Gaelic roots of Scottish kingship. But,
building on nineteenth-century source studies, twentieth-
century Scottish historians and writers opened up the Norse
inheritance of settlement and saga, which belongs to much
of northern and western Scotland. Novelists John Buchan
and Eric Linklater were pioneers in this field, followed by
Naomi Mitchison and George Mackay Brown. Neil Gunn,
who came from Helmsdale in Sutherland, also traced in
fictional form the interaction of Norse and Celtic influences
in a region which represents, to Scots, the far north but, to
Norse peoples, a southern land. More recently, the playwright George Gunn established the Grey Coast Theatre
Company in Caithness in order to give a cultural community
within Scotland back its own narratives in a series of plays,
such as *Songs of the Grey Coast* (1992) and *Gold of Kildonan*
(1989). Gunn also began to explore the dramatic potential
of the Norse sagas, just as Linklater and Mackay Brown
imitated their narrative strengths. This refreshing multi-
culturalism reintroduced to the Scottish cultural pool a
major stream of storytelling influence and tradition. Based
on two or three centuries of oral storytelling, the dense
descriptive and psychological economy of the anonymous
saga makers is a main plank of European narrative art. In the
shape of works like the *Orkneynga Saga*, the Norse narratives
are integral to Scottish literature and storytelling.[13]

Scottish theatre in general drew narrative strength and dramatic interest from the twentieth-century's desire to revisit Scotland's past in new and more questioning ways. Plays such as Stewart Conn's *The Burning (1970)*, based on James VI's interest in witchcraft, and Donald Campbell's *The Jesuit* (1976), based on the trial and execution in 1615 of the Jesuit priest John Ogilvie, evoked powerfully and directly major historical and psychological conflicts. At the same time, the plays reflect contemporary preoccupations. Like Arthur Miller in *The Crucible,* Conn places the witchcraft hunt in the context of power politics, while the Reformation conflict of *The Jesuit* continued to resonate in twentieth-century Scotland when John Ogilvie was beatified and then canonised by the Roman Catholic Church. Both plays became central to the literary revival of Scottish theatre in the late twentieth century. Revising accepted readings of the Scottish past or challenging complacent presumptions is also integral to the work of playwrights such as Hector MacMillan, whose *Royal Visit* (1974) dissects the pageantry of George IV's state visit to Scotland in 1822, while George Rosie's *Carlucco and the Queen of Hearts* (1991), portrays an unbonny Prince Charles in his later years. Sue Glover's *Straw Chair* (1988) and *Bondagers (1991),* which put the missing dimension of female experience back into Scotland's sense of its past, can be seen in the same context.

But storytelling as historical revision was elevated into a theatre-making rationale and method by John McGrath's touring company, 7:84 Scotland. In his ground-breaking *The Cheviot, The Stag and the Black, Black Oil* (1973), McGrath created a hard-hitting politicised storytelling style, based on a mix of music hall, folk tradition and satiric review. A giant pop-up storybook designed by John Byrne provided a mobile narrative backdrop. Stereotypes were not so much challenged as rubbished and recycled for highly effective political ammunition. The touchstone of John McGrath's approach was to recognise that a reworked narrative needs a reworked medium and new audiences[14] and 7:84 Scotland took its work to clubs, pubs and factories where people, whose culture had been marginalised by mainstream middle-class theatre, were ready to engage with both the medium and the message. This kind of flexibility was not so available to film makers during this period but the twenty-first-century impact of video and Internet broadcasting are revolutionising access to storytelling by means of moving pictures.

In the impulse to create imagined worlds, Scottish story-makers in literature and film were not restricted to revisions of Scottish history but also drew on world history, anthropology, philosophy and science. The urge to make narratives into possible worlds and possible worlds into narratives is strongly exemplified in the work of Alasdair Gray whose recreation of Glasgow as an imaginative territory is centred in his epic novel *Lanark* (1981). American bookstores have a similar problem to English literary critics in defining Scottish literature and often classify *Lanark* in the fantasy section. But *Lanark* is a Romance in the medieval sense of the term, fashioned for the twentieth century from a similar mix of psychological realism, philosophical insight, socio-political thought and Utopian fantasy. Similar interests can be combined in science fiction as in the work of Lewis Grassic Gibbon who produced science fiction (also influenced by his anthropological interests) and historical novels under his own name, Leslie Mitchell. In drama, playwright Tom McGrath used social realism, Romance forms and science fiction worlds to pursue a common core of creative interests. In a typical late twentieth-century combination, Iain Banks produced alternatively science fiction as Iain M. Banks and contemporary thriller-romances in his own name, so satisfying the genre expectations of the market place while demonstrating a symmetry of creative intention.

Just as history and fantasy overlap in the making of possible worlds, so the hetero-cosmic instinct overlaps with social criticism and moral insight. Like Lewis Grassic Gibbon (or Leslie Mitchell) in *Spartacus* (1933), Allan Massie used Roman history as a fertile source of alternative worlds, combining a series of fictionalised memoirs for the Julo-Claudian emperors, but Massie's classical narratives sit alongside his exploration of twentieth-century politics

and morality in a series of novels set in post-war Europe.[15]
Novelists such as Robin Jenkins, George Friel, Ian Crichton
Smith and Janice Galloway used realistic and expressionist
techniques to examine the underlying moral nature of
Scottish society and to express a compassionate sense of
individual humanity. Though the forms and techniques
deployed by these writers are often different from the
historical novelists and romancers, their concerns can be
remarkably similar. This is demonstrated by the work of a
writer such as Fred Urquhart, whose historical storymaking
is determinedly realistic and vividly expressive of moral
contradictions in Scottish society. Ian Crichton Smith's
Consider the Lilies (1968) uses a first person realistic narrative to touch the raw nerves of a collective historic experience of clearance. *Consider the Lilies* became a standard text
in Scottish schools and a series of theatre adaptations
provoked a strong emotional response from modern audiences, so heightening political concern about land ownership.

This commonality of concern is unsurprising, given the
shared background of intellectual inquiry and social
thought which characterised Scotland from the medieval
to the modern period. Nineteenth- and twentieth-century
thinkers as diverse as J. G. Frazer, William Robertson Smith,
Patrick Geddes, John Macmurray, A. S. Neill, R. D. Laing,
George Davie, Alasdair MacIntyre and R. F. Mackenzie have
sustained an Enlightenment tradition of philosophical and
social criticism alongside the advances of experimental
science, in which Scottish experimenters have also played
a notable part.[16] A distinctive version of northern European
humanism, tested in the fires of historical experience,
underpins much of Scotland's twentieth-century renaissance
in literature, drama and film.

However, this underlying sense of value or tradition
embraced diversity rather than a monolithic or hierarchical
ordering. Cairns Craig draws on the literary philosophy of
the Russian critic M. M. Bakhtin to characterise Scottish
traditions as a diversity of voices in dialogue and dramatic
tension:

The nature of a national imagination, like a language, is an unending series of interactions between different strands of tradition, between influences from within and without, between the impact of new experiences and the reinterpretation of past experiences: the nation is a series of ongoing debates, founded in institutions and patterns of life, whose elements are continuously changing but which constitute, by the nature of the issues which they foreground, and by their reiteration of elements of the past, a dialogue which is unique to that particular place. The national imagination is not some transcendental identity which either survives or is erased: it is a space in which a dialogue is in process between the various pressures and inheritances that constitute the particularity of human experience in a territory whose boundaries might have been otherwise, but whose borders define the limits within which certain voices, both past and present, with all their centripetal and centrifugal implications, are listened for, and others resisted, no matter how loud they may be.[17]

Combining this approach with the moral philosophy of John Macmurray, Craig argues that cultural traditions can only comprise people interacting and relating to each other, and that the wider, conceptual and imaginative frameworks should not be accorded a metaphysical status apart from their human creators and interpreters.

This model suits modern Scottish culture because of its humanism and because of the diversity of voices, languages and dialects which inform its literature. Central to the twentieth-century renaissance was a denial of the kind of linguistic hegemony accorded to formal English prose by Walter Scott. Instead, novelists as varied as Lewis Grassic Gibbon, Neil Gunn, Nan Shepherd, James Kelman and Janice Galloway shaped different forms and styles in response to the communal and personal voices of the people about whom they wrote. The omniscient external narrator, whose ambiguities had already been exposed by James Hogg in *The Confessions of a Justified Sinner* and R. L. Stevenson in *The Master of Ballantrae* (1888), was supplanted by the experiences of women, of working class rural and urban Scots, and of geographical and cultural minorities whose perspectives had not previously found appropriate literary expression. This surge of new voices and new energies invaded twentieth-century poetry, drama, short stories, novels, television and film, and swept away the standard literary English and received pronunciation which had so inappropriately come to dominate official Scottish culture since the emergence of Victorian gentility. In this way, twentieth-century writers reconnected with what the literary critic Roderick Watson describes as:

> a dialectic between written and spoken discourse with the Scots literary tradition tending to side, much more often than not, with the speed, flexibility and passion of spoken discourse (with its roots in vernacular Scots) as opposed to the more formal registers of written English. And that oral energy was even carried over into discourse in English – most notably, for example, in the eighteenth- and early nineteenth-century prose of Boswell, Hogg, Galt and Carlyle.[18]

The remarkable result of these developments was that oral voices were once more heard in the public arena, reflected in literature, drama and film, and unmediated in their own right. Yet the presumption must be that two and a half centuries of bookish culture, communal dislocation and a century of universal formal education should have put paid to oral traditions. The survival and apparent renaissance of oral song and story in the twentieth century repays close examination, since it underpins a sense of continuity which increased rather than diminished as the century progressed.

The collection and study of Gaelic song and story was continuous from John Francis Campbell's immense labours in the mid-nineteenth century. Among his colleagues and successors were Alexander Carmichael, who produced the five-volume *Carmina Gadelica* (1928–54), Father Allan Mac Donald of Eriskay, Sir Archibald Campbell, who co-edited *Waifs and Strays of Celtic Tradition* (1889–95) with the folklorist

Alfred Nutt, and the ministers Rev. James MacDougall, Rev. Donald MacInnes and the Rev. J. G. Campbell. This scholarly tradition was developed in the twentieth century by the sensitive and meticulous scholarship of John Lorne Campbell of Canna, who was the first collector to use a tape recorder in Scotland.[19] Campbell also linked Scottish oral tradition with the still thriving culture of Gaelic speaking communities in Cape Breton and Nova Scotia. His work established a new benchmark by placing traditional materials in their all-important historical and cultural settings, rather than raiding indigenous cultures for the sake of international cross-references and anthropological theorising.

But the pivotal figure in the recovery and preservation of Gaelic tradition in the twentieth century was Calum Maclean, whose intense twenty years of collecting yielded transcriptions and recordings in the Irish Folklore Commission in Dublin and the School of Scottish Studies in Edinburgh which contain many thousands of tales. Calum Maclean's methods were based on the best scholarly practice but he was animated by political conviction and by a spiritual passion which marked him out and won respect from the communities amongst whom he worked. A fine singer in his own right, Calum Maclean was recognised and accepted as a conduit of the best that Gaelic tradition had to offer.

Maclean was born on the island of Raasay in 1915 and studied Celtic languages at Edinburgh University. In 1939, he went to University College Dublin on a scholarship and, at the outbreak of war, was attracted to Connemara where he began to gather local traditions, later under the auspices of the Irish Folklore Commission. This material is now collected in six manuscript volumes and contains heroic and international tales in the classical mode, and local lore and tradition. In addition, Calum Maclean collected songs, including the contemporary compositions of Páhdraic Ó Fínneadha, which he compared to the *bardachd* or local poetry of his own Hebridean background:

There still are, in the Gaelic-speaking areas of both Ireland and Scotland, local poets about whom very little is known in the outside world. They compose poems and songs which are rarely, if ever, written down. The people of the district learn them by heart, however, and sing them by the fireside, and thus they become known throughout the district. It is seldom that they spread beyond the local confines because they are of interest mainly to the poet's neighbours. The compositions of such poets may not win much acclaim as poetry; still, their works are of interest and even importance since they give us an insight not only into the mind of the poets themselves but also into that of the local people .The Poet of Lochan (Ó Fínneadha) needs no apology or introduction as his poems and songs are already part of the lore of his neighbours. They are sung by the firesides in Cois Fharraige (South Connemara) and they would live on even if they were never written down. Páhdraic Ó Fínneadha was born at a time when history was being made in Ireland (Land War years of the late nineteenth century); that is why even people outside of Cois Fharraige will be interested in his songs, since his outlook was wider than is normally the case with local poets.[20]

In 1945, Calum Maclean was appointed to the full-time staff of the Irish Folklore Commission and was sent as a collector to Scotland, since the Commission recognised that the aristocratic Gaelic social order had survived longer in Scotland than in Ireland. The irony of an independent Ireland acting to safeguard the distinctive cultural heritage of British Scotland cannot have been lost on nationalists such as Calum Maclean. In 1951, the School of Scottish Studies in Edinburgh began, in a modest way, to emulate the Commission's work. Calum Maclean was generously transferred 'on loan' to Scotland along with the gift of a microfilm copy of all the Scottish materials in the Irish archive.

Among the tradition bearers recorded in Scotland by Calum Maclean before his death in 1960 are some outstanding storytellers who deployed all the riches of the Hero Tales, the Wonder Tales and Romances, Clan stories and more recent stories concerning clearance, emigration and war. Such a storyteller was Angus MacMillan of Griminish in

Benbecula. A manuscript collection of his recorded stories amounts to five thousand pages, as well as a three-hundred-page autobiography. Angus MacMillan could not read or write but some of his longer Romances took from seven to nine hours to narrate. By contrast, Calum Maclean's recordings of John Macdonald of Lochaber, an early informant, are a mixture of longer tales with a wealth of local lore and history. For Maclean, John MacDonald was the repository and guardian of his area's heritage, including every battle and clan feud since the fifteenth century! But it is in South Uist that Calum Maclean found a depth and variety of oral tradition unrivalled in either Ireland or Scotland. Among the storytellers and singers of Uist, Duncan Macdonald of Peninerine stands out as a master artist whose language and formal style of delivery are redolent of the older courtly culture with which his family had been connected. The perceptive attention paid by Calum Maclean to Duncan MacDonald reveals his deep regard for the artistic strengths of oral storytelling as an imaginative medium in its own right.[21]

Like all collectors, Calum Maclean was driven by a desire to record cultural riches which were threatened with extinction because of social change and the weakening of oral transmission. But, for Maclean and his informants, the act of gathering was not historical research but a declaration of cultural values based on a belief that their recordings and transcriptions would play some role in the future. The distinctiveness of Gaelic culture, its close relationship with the natural environment, its spirituality, the passion for justice and equality formed by persecution and oppression, the affirmation of a humanity lived out in community: these are values embedded in the oral traditions to which Calum Maclean devoted his exceptional life. On his death in 1960, Calum Maclean was eulogised by his brother, the poet Sorley Maclean, in a traditional elegy:

> There is many a poor man in Scotland
> whose spirit and name you raised;
> you lifted the humble

whom our age put aside.
They gave you more
than they would give to others
since you gave them the zeal
that was a fire beneath your kindness.
They sensed the vehemence
that was gentle in your ways,
They understood the heavy depths of your humanity
when your fun was at its lightest.

You are talked of in Cois Fhairrge
over in Ireland:
between Cararoe and Spideal
you left many a knot.
You were to the Gaels of Ireland
as one of themselves and of their people.
They knew in you the humanity
that the sea did not tear,
that a thousand years did not spoil;
the quality of the Gael permanent.

You proved in Shetland
and in Sweden
and in Norway
that there is no bitterness in the sea:
that the 'malice' is only a word
that chokes lasting truth.
Since you were a favourite with the Gael
you were a favourite with the Gall.
Since you cared for the man
and did not know guile
or sleekitness or fawning for place,
you made Gaels of the Galls.

That iomadh duine bochd an albainn
dh'an tug thu togail agus cliù;
s ann a thog thu'n t-iriosal
a chuir ar linn air chùl.
Thug iad dhutsa barrachd

na bheireadh iad do chàch
on thug thu dhaibh an dùrachd
bu ghrìosach fo do bhàigh.
Mhothaich iadsan an dealas
a bha socair'na do dhòigh
thuig iad doimhne throm do dhaondachd
nuair a b'aotroime do spòrs.

Tha sgeul ort an Cois-Fhairge
ann an Erinn thall:
eadar an Ceathramh Ruadh is Spideal
dh'fhàg thu iomadh snaim.
Bha thu aig Gàidheil Eirinn
mar fhear dhiubh fhéin's de'n dream.
Dh'aithnich iad annad-sa an fhéile
nach do reub an cuan,
nach domhill mìle bliadhna:
buaidh a'Ghàidheal buan

Dhearbh thu ann an Sealtainn
agus anns an t-Suain
agus ann an Lochlann
nach eil seirbhe anns a'chuan;
nach eil'sa'ghamlas ach facal
a thachdas fìrinn bhuan.
On bu mhùirnean thu do'n Ghàidheal
bu mhùirnean thu do'n Ghall.
Onbha t'ùidh anns an duine
s nach b'aithne dhut an fhoill
no sliomaireachd no sodal stàite,
rinn thu Gàidheil dhe na Goill.[22]

Calum Malean's legacy endured in the work of colleagues
and successors such as John MacInnes, Donald Archie Mac-
Donald, Alan Bruford and John Shaw. But it also reflected
back to the Gaelic-speaking community a sense of significance
and value which had been systematically eroded by the ex-
clusion of Gaelic from formal education since the eighteenth
century. Just as in the late nineteenth century the Gaelic

community had begun to fight back on the land issue, so, in the late twentieth century, language and culture became the touchstones of recovery. The fight back was led by music, song and the poetry of established literary artists such as Sorley Maclean and Derick Thomson, as well as the *bardachd* of local poets such as Donald John MacDonald of Uist and Iain MacNeacail of Skye – the Skipper. Storytelling has only tentatively found a place in this twentieth-century renaissance but the recovery of storytelling in contemporary forms is a key to the sustainable community of language which Gaelic will need to survive the twenty-first century. As a third millennium began, the Tobar an Dualchais project began transferring the fruit of Calum Maclean's heroic efforts on to the Internet as a resource and stimulus for any community or storytelling artist in Scotland and beyond.

From the inception of the School of Scottish Studies in 1951, Calum Maclean had a partner and collaborator in the shape of Hamish Henderson. A Perthshire Scot who had attended Blairgowrie High School and Cambridge University, Henderson's interest in folk tradition was whetted by war service in which he experienced the songs and barrack-room ballads of the Eighth Army and, as an intelligence officer, the music of the Italian resistance. At the same time, Henderson nurtured literary ambitions, producing in *Elegies for the Dead in Cyrenaica* (1948) some of World War II's finest poetry.

As early as 1946, Hamish Henderson was advocating the systematic collection and study of Scots folksong as part of a radical agenda for the democratisation of the Scottish literary renaissance. In this cause, he was later to famously take on the more aloof Hugh MacDiarmid in an extended flyting or controversy.[23] Henderson's agenda led not just to the emergence of the School of Scottish Studies on a shoe-string budget, but to the first Edinburgh People's Festival in 1951 – a precursor of both the Edinburgh Festival Fringe and later Folk Festivals. During the People's Festival, traditional folk artists were linked up with community groups, trade unions and political campaigners. This was the antithesis of the nineteenth-century 'drawing room' revival of folk tradition that had been spawned by Sir Walter Scott and his literary successors. The contemporary social and political context were critical motivating factors for both Maclean and Henderson. At this time the latter was also engaged in translating the prison letters of the Italian Marxist and cultural commentator, Antonio Gramsci.[24]

However, none of this agenda would have made the impact it did without the rediscovery of a living oral tradition. The stream of tradition had been sustained by socially and politically marginalised groups such as farm workers, Gaelic speaking crofters and, supremely for Henderson, the Scottish Travellers – a still nomadic ethnic minority, condemned for centuries by settled society as 'tinklers' and 'gypsies'. Such traditions were not a matter of cultural taste but of social function, if not survival. Hence the cultural and political lesson for a wider Scottish society, which was only gradually recovering its own identity and self-confidence.

The strength of Hamish Henderson's case was powerfully demonstrated by the 'discovery' of the Traveller folk artist, Jeannie Robertson, in an Aberdeen council house in 1953.[25] Jeannie Robertson's artistry was to gain international recognition through concerts and recordings, while her home became an informal academy of folk tradition, welcoming and educating scholars and the impressionable young alike. Jeannie's texts and renditions of classic ballads such as 'The Gypsy Laddie' became defining, because they were being shaped within a still fluid tradition of oral composition. Each performance seemed to dig into a deep possibility of recreation. This was because, although Jeannie herself made a personal transition from being an artist within her tradition to an interpreter of that tradition in a wider context, her art remained rooted within the centuries-old cultural loyalties and customs of the Scottish Travellers:

> Three Gypsies came tae oor hall door,
>   An' O but they sang bonnie, O;
> They sang so sweet and too complete
>   That they stole the hairt of our lady O.

For she cam' tripping down the stair,
   Her maidens two before her O;
And when they sa' her weel-faur'd face
   They throw'd their spells oot owre her O.

When her good lord came home that night,
   He was askin' for his lady;
The answer the servants gave tae him:
   'She's awa' wi' the Gypsy laddies O.'

'Gae saddle tae me my bonnie bonnie black,
   The broun it's ne'er sae speedie O;
That I may go ridin'; this long summer day
   In search of my true lady O.'
         [. . .]
'For the very last night I crossed this river
   I had dukes and lords to attend me O;
But this night I must put in my warm feet an' wyde
   An' the gypsies wydin' before me O.'

'Last night I lay in a good feather bed,
   And my own weddit lord beside me O;
But this night I must lie in a caald corn-barn
   An' the Gypsies lyin' aroond me O.'

'For it's will you give up your houses and your land,
   And will you give up your baby O?
And will you give up your own weddit lord
   And keep follyin' the Gypsy laddies O?'

'For it's I'll give up my houses and my land,
   And I'll give up my baby O;
And I'll give up my own weddit lord
   And keep follyin' the Gypsy laddies O.'

'For they are seven brothers of us all,
   We are all wondrous bonnie O;
And this very night we all shall be hanged
   For the stealin' of the earl's lady O.'[26]

This narrative is clearly shaped on the frontier between settled and Traveller society and skilfully interweaves the different voiceprints of the servants, the lord, the lady and finally the gypsy brothers, who must be hanged to reassert the primacy of the propertied, law-enforcing order. But, as delivered by Jeannie 'The Gypsy Laddie' becomes a passionate lament and protest on behalf of the Traveller culture which transcends rather than transgresses the social order, because it aspires to the freedom of nature. The gypsies of this classic ballad become the Travellers of Jeannie Robertson's own family traditions – oppressed and blamed for being themselves outside the nature/culture demarcation of the settled Scots. The last stanza is a powerful and ironic reprise of the first stanza with the repetition of 'bonnie', 'wondrous' for 'so sweet and too complete,' and 'stealin' of the earl's lady O' for 'they stole the hairt of our lady O'. The economy of implication is superb and the language is taut, pointed and dramatic even without the emotional punch of sung melody.

The frontier status of Jeannie Robertson's 'The Gypsy Laddie' points to the significance of this art not just in Traveller society but for Scotland as a whole. The transcending of old boundaries and prejudices is underlined by Jeannie Robertson's and the Travellers' preservation of classic, historical ballads such as 'The Battle of Harlaw'. To hear Jeannie's version of 'Harlaw' was to receive an eye witness account of this vital clash between Highland and Lowland power in 1411:

> As I cam' by the Garioch land
>   An' doun by Netherha';
> There were fifty thoosan' Hielan'men
>   A-marchin' tae Harlaw.
> Refrain:
> Singin' diddie-aye-O
> Sing fa-la-doh
> Sing diddie-aye-O-aye-ay.
> 'It's did ye come fae the Hielan's, man,
>   An did ye come a' the wey?
> An' did ye see MacDonal' an' his men
>   As they marched tae Skye?'[27]

Whatever its eye-witness status, 'The Battle of Harlaw' is a composition of that period passed on in oral tradition. As Calum Maclean pointed out, not everything is contained in the written history.

It was more than a year after Hamish Henderson's first encounter with Jeannie Robertson that he experienced her additional gift as a storyteller and, in 1954, he recorded his first Scots Traveller folk tale, 'Silly Jack and the Lord's Daughter'[28] from Jeannie. A similar pattern followed in the late fifties and sixties with other Traveller tradition bearers, including the Stewarts of Blair, Stanley Robertson and Duncan Williamson, who all first came to attention as traditional singers and were then revealed to be storytellers as well. The significance of this development was that the Scots folk tale was generally believed to have died out in its oral form. John Francis Campbell suggested this in his 1860 introduction to *Popular Tales of the West Highlands*, while Robert Chambers' stories in *Popular Rhymes of Scotland* (1826) seem to have come to him in manuscript form from earlier collectors, such as Peter Buchan and Charles Kirkpatrick Sharpe. No-one had challenged this presumption until, a century later, this welling stream of Traveller storytelling was uncovered.

Storytelling, like ballad-singing, was not pursued as an abstract art among Travellers but as a craft, bearing the moral and spiritual values of their culture, and as a primary form of entertainment. Storytelling was tied in with family relationships, since particular families and family members told particular stories. Younger people inherited stories from older family members. Because these stories reflected their individual experiences and characters, alongside communal values, the passing on of a story became a bond between family members. In her collection of Perthshire folk tales, *The King of the Black Art*, Sheila Douglas describes the context of storytelling as a web of family connection:

> It is important however to remember that the family circle of my storytellers, like that of all Travellers, is a much wider one than those of the settled people, and more reminiscent of

the old Highland clan. Two of my storytellers and two of their daughters have become world famous as the Stewarts of Blair and people may assume that this was the sum total of the family. But as well as two daughters, they had two sons and another daughter, as well as brothers and sisters, aunts, uncles and cousins and countless other relatives: not so much a family tree as a family forest, in which the Stewarts of Blair are but a twig! Moreover, the Stewarts were inextricably bound up with MacPhees, MacGregors, Higginses, Reids and many other traveller clans, so that one can begin to appreciate the truth of the saying , 'tinkers are aa sib'. The four storytellers whose stories appear in this book are Alec and Belle Stewart, Alec's younger brother John and their cousin Willie MacPhee.[29]

At the time of writing in 1987, these four senior family members were the bearers of a rich storytelling tradition, embracing international tales (some drawn from Gaelic sources), Jack tales, Burker stories, humorous and dramatic anecdotes or *Schwänken,* and accounts of Traveller life and experience. Alongside the stories, family members sang and made music. The main exponent of this family's tradition is now Sheila Stewart, daughter of Alec and Belle.[30]

A similar pattern can be traced amongst the Sutherland Travellers, who were also recorded in the 1950s by Hamish Henderson, and by Calum Maclean since Gaelic was still their primary language. At the centre of the Sutherland network was Alexander Stewart of Lairg, Ailidh Dall, a tinsmith, piper, soldier, singer and storyteller with a repertoire that ran wide and deep, including Fenian Hero Tales and Arthurian ballad. Ailidh Dall's granddaughter, Essie Stewart, continues to share this repertoire, as well as stories from the pearl-fishing Davies clan of her husband, Eddie, and the Ross-shire Williamsons with whom the Stewarts are also intermarried.[31]

But, paradoxically, as exposure to Traveller culture and storytelling increased, the distinctive Traveller lifestyle was eroding as the need for peddlers and itinerant labour diminished and social pressure to settle and school became more systematic. A number of storytellers began to emerge as individual artists and as interpreters of the Traveller culture to a wider public. One of the first of these was Betsy Whyte from Montrose, whose modest self-contained manner belied a vivid descriptive imagination, expressed through sure concision and grace in narration. A recording of Betsy Whyte, made at the School of Scottish Studies in 1987, demonstrates the clarity of her gift and the bridge-building between Traveller and 'scaldie', or settled, culture which had by then become natural to her:

> Dae ye ken what a Broonie is? No? Well, in Scotland we have a Broonie, a spirit creature – not only fairies an witches an waarlocks an aa that kind o things but we also have the Broonie. But the Broonie wis a very helpful spirit, an it couldn't take on a very nice form. It used tae look terrible, an everybody was frightened o it, and it kept away oot o the sight o people if it could. It was mostly covered in brown hair like a coconut; it had iron teeth, and its eyes were the same as they'd been half plucked out and tried to be . . . pushed back in again! An its feet were at least a yard in length – so that everybody was terrified o the Broonie. But they'd nae reason to be, it never – a Broonie wis never haerd tae dae any harm tae anybody.[32]

Having established a context of common understanding, Betsy delineates her tale with swift economy:

> Now, near this place there lived a young miller, an he lived wi's mother. An his mother dabbled aboot in the Black Art an witchcraft an charms an aa that kind o thing, an this young fella, he was her only son. An there wis a fairmer's daughter, an she would have gave anything for him. She really cared aboot him. But he wis courtin a servant lassie on another fairm. Now his mother wisnae very pleased at that, she thought he should ha' took this fairmer's daughter, an she said, 'Look,' she says, 'a big fairm an everything, an it would be yours, because her father's getting on a bit now.'

He says, 'I cannae help it, mother,' he said. He says, 'I love Katie,' he said, 'an A'm gaunnae marry Katie.'

She says, 'Ye're naw gaunnae marry the fairmer's daughter!'

He says, 'Never, mother!' He said, 'A'm gaunnae marry Katie, the servant lassie.'[33]

The transition here from exposition to development is seamless, effected through the switch from the attitude of the mother, to her speech, to dramatic dialogue, all over a few lines. The tale is then pursued to its end with such a concentrated unerring flow that the listener must stay with it until released.

Many of the same skills are evident in Betsy Whyte's autobiographical memoirs, particularly *Yellow on the Broom (1979)*. There, similarly concision and vivid descriptive language combine with shrewd psychological insight and patent sincerity. The memoir is a manifestation of what Ruskin called the 'intelligent heart' laying itself open to the listener in order to share a truth of nature. *Yellow on the Broom* reaffirms throughout that the sensations, emotions and instincts of close companionship with the natural world were central to Traveller lifestyle:

The men were pearl-fishing the river. I soon found my way there too, and walked along the path on the bank. I wondered, as I walked, why there nearly always was a path along river banks. No matter how isolated the river was, one could always find a path along the bank. Rounding a bend on the river, I suddenly stopped and stared. It was so beautiful. Masses of forget-me-nots bordered the river, almost into the water. May flowers carpeted the banks and fragile-looking wood anemones, which would rather die than live anywhere but under their beloved trees, grew in profusion in the wooded area. Many other species of wild flowers were also to be seen, and their mingled scents were so pleasing. I filled my eyes with the beauty around me, and breathed deeply the wonderful scents. Oh this is so good, I thought, after the stour and noise of the mill.

I found a green patch and lay down on my belly on the cool green grass. It was a very warm day and numerous sounds of nature filled my ears. The husky, yet somehow high-pitched, whispering whistle of a mouse told me that it had a nest of young down there somewhere near. The sound of grasshoppers, jumping-jacks we called them, and the gentle rustle of a nearby shaking ash tree. What secret of nature made the leaves of this tree rustle, when every other tree was still and quiet? Was it the gossip of the woods, whispering about its friends and neighbours? The river, too, seemed to whisper and mumble as it glided past. I lay there in a state of ecstasy . . .

So I was more than annoyed when I felt the ground moving under me. 'god pity you, you silly wee black moudie!' I said aloud. I know that if he could burrow through the hard ground, then he could easily burrow through my soft body. Not that I ever heard of any such thing, but I was not going to lippen on it.

So I got up rather hastily and found that it was several minutes before my eyes would focus properly and before the earth would stop spinning under my feet. So deeply had my emotions been spellbound with so much beauty.[34]

It is significant that, even in this extended description and recall, the form is a narrative one which opens with the arrival of the experiencing 'I' and closes with her departure. Betsy Whyte's description is echoed in Stanley Robertson's account in *Exodus to Alford (1988)* of his family setting out on the road in 1946 after World War II to travel their old routes along the Dee and the Don:

My little brother and I sat on the back of the cart, surrounded by all the things we most valued in our lives . . . my sisters and other women folk trekked along the road, the great excitement in their voices mellowing and flowing in the gentle breezes . . . Songs rendered the air and so did stories of the past . . . The men often stopped for a smoke or to take tea provided by the womenfolk along the route . . . Everything was wonderful!

153

To the country people we passed we may have seemed a strange migration, but to us this was a journey to a better land – where we would be at home again with the natural elements to whom we belonged – and where for generations we had been a part of that creation and at home within it . . . and so as we were now far away from the eye of the scaldies, we felt a deep sense of privacy and a feeling of pure freedom.[35]

A nephew of Jeannie Robertson, Stanley Robertson, inherited songs and stories from a range of family members and he has developed a widely recognised expertise in the balladry and oral narrative of Traveller tradition. A favourite tale is Stanley's story about Auld Cruivie, an ancient gnarled oak on the Old Lumphanan Road. The Old Road was a prized summer camping ground and haven for the Robertson family and Stanley draws on family tradition when he invests this landscape with magical significance:

[The Old Road of Lumphanan] is our little kingdom in between. An tae the left you've the Don and tae the right you've the Dee. An my mither aye said, she says, "The Black Don is the warlock and the Dee's the witch, the silvery Dees's the witch. An . . . the twa are the man an wife, an the land in between is for us. That's oor land." And that land oddly enough lies directly right aroon the hill [by the Old Road] an richt enough the whole area is surrounded. It is a kingdom on its own.[36]

On midsummer eve, Auld Cruivie uproots himself to dance with the other trees by the river. Beneath his roots is treasure and, if Jack the hero can manage at the right time to climb and retrieve just some of that treasure – but not too much – he will make his own and his poor widowed mother's fortune. But the wicked laird – a laird of the black art – wants all the treasure for himself, even if it means sacrificing Jack to be buried alive. But a young serving lassie who has fallen in love with Jack outwits the laird and rescues him. The main treasure is preserved and Jack has made his fortune but in a way that restores rather than subverts the natural order of renewal, the moral order of good and evil, and the magical order of increase versus destruction. Jack and we, the listeners, have learnt a lesson by being initiated into several layers of life experience. As Stanley comments:

> Well, tae me, Jack fan he's travellin is jus' like the travellin people's aspirations an their dreams an their hopes an potentials, an that in Jack [tales] they could see how Jack's progression, fit Jack's daein tae come from rags tae riches he aye retains things that he had; he aye treasures the things that he had at the beginning . . . He very seldom throws awa his auld roots.[37]

Stanley Robertson is a complex artist, moving in a range of works between the oral tradition and conscious creation, but at the centre of all his storytelling is a philosophic under-standing of Traveller culture and values. This is particularly apparent in his handling of fear. As both philosopher/artist and a compulsive entertainer, Stanley returns again and again to experiences of supernatural fear:

> 'Indian Death' is a term that I use and ma granny an ma mither used for when you go to your bed at night an suddenly you waken up and the room's icy cold, an things happen an you're aware of it. I could get up, say, . . . let's jist say like this, we're recording here and I maybe jist close my eyes for a second, an I fall asleep – I kin' of waken up like that. Barbara would be sittin there; the tape recorder would be gaun roond; you would be sittin there; Heather would still be doon there playin with her cards, but the room would be icy cold. An A'd say tae myself, 'Have I fell asleep or am I in an Indian Death?' And then – 'at's aa richt, but it's fit comes in 'e door, 'is is the horror, it's whit comes intae the door! Sometimes you get wonderful experiences, but there's times when you get horrific [ones] – and fan I say horrific I mean horrific! It could be a wakin dream, but tae me – I think ye're jist hittin anither dimension. 'Ken, I think there's a dimen-sion in . . . people's mind that's never been opened.[38]

As this autobiographical comment shows, a sense of the supernatural – good and evil – is seen by Stanley Robertson as a characteristic of Traveller culture and is prominent in his interpretation of Traveller ballads and stories. In performance, Stanley uses this sense to eerie, tragic and, sometimes, to comic effect. Supernatural experience is, for Stanley, the validation of a dimension which he believes central to human existence. It is as vitally necessary to confront fear and to name the demons and spirits, as it is to learn the lessons of loyalty and human decency. This must be seen in the context of an ethnic group which was familiar with psychic gifts, and prey not just to psychological fears but to the attentions of body-snatchers and other 'scaldie' oppressors. Again the tales have an educative and therapeutic value for Traveller culture and for a wider Scottish society in which the Calvinist legacy of supernatural awe, guilt and fear seems to fade insensibly into a shallow materialistic apathy, reluctant to confront either its angels or its demons. Scottish and Traveller tales bridge the gaps between literature's divided selves in a way this is in tune with an underlying ethic of acceptance and healing.

Each of the great Traveller storytellers has their own distinctive character and artistic approach. When Sheila Stewart of Blairgowrie tells stories she taps a vein of fantasy and rich dramatic humour which belongs to her family tradition, but she also employs a verve and gusto – a force of personality and language – which is entirely her own: there is tradition and the individual talent. Perhaps, though, the Stewarts as a family group are closest to the Traveller tradition of stories as a superb form of entertainment – the best possible way to while away long periods of time whose rhythm depends on the vagaries of nature and the weather. Willie MacPhee, piper, tinsmith and storyteller, is a supreme exponent of narrative as a relaxation in which serious messages are not allowed to spoil the fun. In a favourite tale 'The Wandering Piper' Willie relates, in dead-pan laid-back style, the fortunes of a poor Traveller who is out in the depth of winter, when he comes across a corpse wearing a fine pair of boots.[39] The only problem is the corpse is frozen and the boots stuck fast, so the adaptable piper takes out his tool kit and chiseling 'roon about the ankler' saws off the feet, boots and all. 'He got the two o them aff an tied them thegither an put them roon his neck an he's away on the road noo.' Next, the piper seeks refuge in a remote cottage but the couple turn him away, eventually relenting and sending him to the byre, alongside the cow whose breath overnight melts the boots:

> So he slept there for a long time. He didnae ken hoo lang he sleppit. He was wakent early in the oors o the mornin, aboot half past six in the mornin, he wakent up. He lucked over an he seen the coo still chowin away. 'I wonder,' he says, 'if my boots is thawed oot yet.'
>
> So he went roon an he got his boots back roond, the dead man's boots. Of coorse the feet came oot dead easy, ye see, oot o the sock, the two o them; he left them doon. 'Oh,' he says, 'that's lovely!' An he tried these boots on an they were lovely and warm wi the coo's breath, ye see. So he laced them ontae his feet. 'Oh,' he says, 'that's lovely. That's beautiful,' he says. 'That's better now. I'll be able to go on the road a bit better noo.'[40]

Then the piper puts the sawn off stumps of feet in his own boots beside the cow and lies back in the straw. The old woman comes to milk the cow:

> 'Oh my God!' she says. 'Oh my God!' she says. 'That was the piper, the wanderin piper,' she says. 'The coo must have ett him!' she says. 'Oh whit am I gonnae do?' She left the stool an left her pail an she run roon tat the hoose again. She tellt her oul man, 'Come oot ae ye see this!' she says. 'Come oot tae see this!'
>
> He says, 'Whit's wrong? Whit's wrong wi ye, silly oul woman?'
>
> 'Come here tae ye see this!' she says. 'The cow's ett the piper,' she says. 'The cow's ett the piper. Come here tae ye see this!'
>
> So of course the fairmer came an he lookit. 'Oh my God Almighty!' he says. 'It did eat him right enough!' he says

'That's his boots,' he says. 'ett him all but his boots. Oh,' he says, 'we're gaun tae get transported!' he says. 'We're gonnae get pit away frae the world when everybody fins us oot. We'll have tae bury these boots,' he says, 'an this bits o feet. But the ground's that hard,' he says, 'I don't know where we're gonnae bury them'.[41]

Having, with difficulty, buried 'the corpse' or at least its boots and feet, the frightened couple return to the house. The piper then blows up a tune and comes marching up the garden – the perfect incarnation of a 'ghostly piper':

So the ould fairmer an his ould wife run away up the road, ye see. So the ould piper came up an he seen them runnin an he stopped an came up tae the hoose an he stood having a good look efter them. He opened the door an come intae the hoose, an of coorse the fire was still burnin, ye see. So he rakit up the fire and he got a good heat and there wis a good drop whisky left in the bottle. The ould piper liftit the whisky, drunk the whisky an had a bit o this chicken. 'Well,' he says, 'maybe that's set them,' he says, 'a lesson, for no lettin people in at nicht.'
So I think the piper's still stuck at that fairm yer. An that's the last o my story. The auld fairmer never came back.[42]

This is a tall tale, black comedy and silent movie all in one! The moral is hardly the main point though it neatly closes the narration. For the duration of the tale we have been eased into timeless suspension but closure returns us to clock time and the pressures of immediate experience.

If Willie MacPhee is an exemplar of Traveller entertainment, Duncan Williamson is an individual artist of a different stamp. Duncan Williamson was born in 1928 into a large family of Argyllshire Travellers, rich in storytelling and music and still close to Gaelic tradition, though Gaelic was no longer their first language. Like the other Traveller artists, Duncan absorbed a wide repertoire of international and Wonder Tales, Jack tales and family stories as a child. One of his early memories is of searching his Granny

MacDonald's purse for the treasure store of stories from which she selected her nightly tales. As a result, the old lady ceased to share or tell her stories.[43] This anecdote is revealing since it appears to instil at an impressionable age the central tenet of Duncan Williamson's mature art: never force the gates of wonder. It also illustrates the way in which, albeit unconsciously, Duncan was from early in life a collector and connoisseur of stories.

On leaving school in Furnace at fourteen, where the family had a settled camp, Duncan was apprenticed to a stonemason and drystane dyker, Neil McCallum, from whom he heard many Gaelic and Argyllshire stories. Hamish Henderson takes up the story:

> When he was fifteen Duncan decided – like Jack in the folktales – to 'push his fortune' out in the wide world; he left home with an older brother and travelled through Argyll, Perthshire, Angus and the Mearns; in subsequent years, with a cousin of his mother's, he roamed as far north as Inverness-shire, and as far south and east as Dumfriesshire and Fife. He worked here and there as a farm labourer and harvester; he also learned the trade of horse-dealing, and became an expert at it. However, in the summer months he would always return to his folk on Loch Fyneside.[44]

This itinerant way of life and contact with a variety of skills and crafts put Duncan in an ideal position to gather stories from all parts of Scotland and he took full advantage of the opportunities. In his collection, *Tales of the Seal People (1992)*, Duncan Williamson prefaces each story with a short account of its source:

> This silkie story was first told to me a long time ago in Argyll by an old gamekeeper and deer stalker called Peter Munro. I used to go with Peter sometimes when he took out his pony. When he shot a deer out on the hill, a big stag, he would need a help to lift the stag onto the back of the pony. He would come by where I was working and ask the old farmer, 'Can I borrow Duncan for an hour?' He would pay me half a

crown, and I always looked forward to this because it was extra money. We were sitting resting one day when I asked about stories, and this is one he told me.

[Wounded Seal][45]

Now this happened to me a long time ago when I was only thirteen years old working with an old fisherman, Duncan Campbell. I think old Duncan had a notion to me because I was called Duncan. He was an elderly man in his late sixties, and he and I used to dig bait together for this fishing. We used to row his little boat from Furnace to Minard at the graveyard there. It was a big beach and if you landed too early you had to wait till the tide went out. As we sat there by the seaside we watched the popping heads of the seals which is a wonderful thing to see. I said, 'Duncan, my friend, there are many strange stories about the seal people.' And he told me this story.

[Silkie's Farewell][46]

Gradually Duncan Williamson came to realise the importance to him of this story instinct and he evolved into a conscious champion of the Travellers' oral culture and an advocate of the wider, social and therapeutic benefits of storytelling. Duncan Williamson was first recorded by Helen Fullerton and the collector Geordie MacIntyre as a ballad singer and poet. Then, from 1968, he appeared at the early Blairgowrie Folk Festivals but it was only after his marriage, following the death of his first wife, to the folklorist Linda Headlee that Duncan's storytelling gifts became more widely known and appreciated.

The starting point of Duncan Williamson's stories may be a deft portrait of a family situation, the setting of an imaginary court or an Argyllshire village or, less usually, a reference to a historical character such as Malcolm Canmore. But the trend of the narrative is always from situation and psychology towards fable. Many of his stories are explicit fables of love and wisdom, rooted in universal values which Duncan believes are characteristic of Traveller culture at its best. In one important group of stories, the central character is a king who has to learn a lesson through the experience of the story. In 'I Love You More Than Salt' – a version of the Lear story – the king must learn that his youngest daughter's apparently terse devotion is, in reality, as true and necessary as salt. In 'The King of the East and the King of the West', the king must learn that a garden close to wild nature is one that gives refuge to biodiversity. In 'The King and the Lamp', the king is taught by a tinker the equivalence between justice and generosity. In 'The Thorn in the King's Foot', the king must learn that love and healing should work together if king and kingdom are to flourish. In 'Give This to the One You Love Best', the king – an enfabled Malcolm Canmore – learns through a disillusioning cycle of gift-giving that the person who really deserves his prized golden bowl is his Fool.[47]

Yet these stories are not moralistic since, at their heart, is a transformation involving exchange between some form of natural or healing power and energy, on the one hand, and human love, on the other. This theme is prominent in Duncan Williamson's silkie stories, which concern dealings between human beings and the seal people. Love may make such exchanges fruitful and enriching for both parties but fear, hate and violence may bring loss and separation: only the courage of true love can enter into the natural/supernatural world of the silkies without fear. Otherwise relationships are broken and the possibilities foreclosed, as when the old fisherman and his wife in 'La Mer, La Moocht' cannot follow the merman into his natural element, the sea:

> An his wife said, 'Please, take him back and set him free.'
> So La Mer and the fisherman walked back to the same rocks where he catcht him, he said, 'La Mer, you're free. Go, La Mer.'
> And La Mer turned round, said, 'Won't you come with me, auld man/come with me to the sea, I'll take ye to a place where you will never need to fish anymore, where there diamonds is an pearls, where the land – you will be free – where everything is a wonderful place.'
> He said, 'I couldn't leave my auld wife.'

'Walk with me,' said la Mer, 'please come with me! Just put your feet in the sea, an I'll take you with me.'

'I'll walk with ye,' said the fisherman, 'I'll see you off, because I don't want tae give you to anyone. Because we love you dearly.'

So 'e auld fisherman walked into the sea with La Mer behind the rocks, and then lo and behold La Mer turnt roond – he catcht the auld fisherman bi the hand – he held on to the fisherman's hand, 'Come with me,' said La Mer. 'Please come with me – you been good to me an you treatit me so square and so wonderful – please come and join me in my land, come, please . . . '

And the auld fisherman went in to his waist, then the auld fisherman went up tae his neck, then the auld fisherman went up tae his head and the water cam in tae his eyes. But La Mer jist was like a fish and the water didna seem to affect him any way. But the water's gaun into the auld fisherman's neck and he begint tae feel that he wis drownin. He said, 'Please, La Mer, please, La Mer, let go your grip – ye're far too strong for me!'

'Come with me,' says La Mer, 'an I'll take you to the bottom o the sea, where you'll never need to worry, where everything is free!'

'Please, please,' said the fisherman, 'let go your grip, ye're far too strong for me!' And then La Mer let go his grip, the auld fisherman walked back to the shoreside and La Mer was gone.

He walkit home and he told his wife. She said, 'Where is La Mer?'

He said, 'La Mer is gone . . . fir evermore, but someday I'll gae back tae the sea.'

She says, 'Look, husband, if you go back to the sea, will ye take me with you?' And that is the end of my story.[48]

Transformation or metamorphosis operates as a defining motif within Duncan Williamson's tales. In 'Tatties from Chuckie-Stanes', a poor Traveller woman puts stones on to boil to ease her children's hunger pangs into sleep. But a passing fairy turns them – on Christmas Eve! – into floury

tatties bursting their skins.[49] In 'Death in a Nut', the hero
Jack wrestles death down into a tiny nut and casts him into
the sea, only to find that this heroic effort to protect his
mother has cancelled all death. The eggs will not break, the
vegetables will not uproot and animals can't be killed: death
is the necessary transformation that gives life. Jack learns to
release and accept the grim reaper, though his mother's life
is spared meantime. Here the fit between the life wisdom of
the tale and its metamorphic motif is perfect.[50]

Duncan Williamson's oral version of the 'Tam Lin' ballad
– sometimes called 'Lady Margaret' – is defining within his
narrative canon:

> Oh Lady Marg'ret she sat in her high chamber, she was
>   sewing her silken seams
> She luikit east an she luikit west, an she saw those woods grow
>   green.
> So picking up her petticoat beneath her harlin gown . . .
> An when she came to the merry green wood, it was there she
>   let it down.
> For she had not pulled one nut, one nut, one nut nor
>   scarcely three,
> When the highest lord in aa the countryside came a-riding
>   through the trees.
> He said, 'why do you pull those nuts, those nuts; how dare
>   you bend those trees!
> How dare you come to this merry green woods without the
>   leave of me!'
> She said, 'Wonst on time those woods were mine, without a
>   leave of yours,
> And I can pull those nuts, those nuts,
> and I sure can bend those trees, those trees
> I sure can bend those trees.'
> So he took her gently by the hand and he gently laid her
>   down;
> And when he had his will of her, he rose her up again.
> She said, 'Now you've had your will of me, come tell to me
>   your name!
> And if a baby I do have, I will call it the same.'

He said, 'I'm an earl's son from Carlisle, and I own all those
    woods so green,
But I was taken when I was young by an evil Fairy Queen.
'But,' he said, 'tomorrow night is Halloween, and all those
    nobles you can see;
And if you will come to the five-mile gate, it is there you can
    set me free, oh free
It is there you can set me free.
Oh first they will come some dark, some dark, and then they
    will come some brown;
But when there comes a milk-white steed, you must pull its
    rider down, down,
You must pull its rider down.
Oh first, I'll turn to a wicked snake and then to a lion so wild,
Oh hold me fast an fear me not, I may be the father of your
    child!
And then I'll turn to a nakit man, oh an angry man I'll be!
Just throw your mantle over me, an then you will have me
    free, oh free,
An then you will have me free!'
So that night at the midnight hour Lady Marg'ret made her
    way
And when she came to the five-mile gate she waitit patiently,
    oh lee,
She waited patiently!
Oh first there came some dark, some dark and then there
    came some brown,
But when there came a milk-white steed, she pulled its rider
    down, down,
She pulled its rider down!
Oh first he turned to a wicked snake and then to a lion so
    wild,
She held him fast an feared him not – he could be the father
    of her child, her child,
Be the father of her child!
Then he changed to a nakit man, oh an angry man was he!
She threw her mantle over him, an then she had him free,
    oh free,
And then she had him free!

Then cried the voice of the Fairy Queen, oh an angry queen
    was she,
Sayin, 'If I had hae known yesterday, oh what I know today
I'd took out your very heart's blood an put in a heart of clay,
    of clay
An put in a hear of clay!'
So Lady Marg'ret on the white-milk steed, Lord William on a
    dapple grey;
With the bugle an the horn hangin down by their sides, it's
    merrily they rode away, away
It's merrily they rode away![51]

This version of 'Tam Lin' is a family one which Duncan first heard from his paternal grandmother, Bet McColl. The use of Lady Margaret and Lord William, lends the Williamson version a concrete starting point. The narrative structure then becomes a revelatory framing sequence which moves from named character to the forbidden wood, to sexual encounter, to supernatural encounter, to conflict and metamorphosis, to human return. Natural power opens into magic and the supernatural, but it is love's courage that wins the day for humanity.

But, to be effective, the transformative nature of the ballad or tale must be reflected in its performance. The teller's commitment to the story and to the audience must be psychologically and emotionally whole-hearted if he or she is to be true to the nature of their art. In their detailed study, *Jeannie Robertson: Emergent Singer, Transformative Voice (1999)*, James Porter and Herschel Gower demonstrate how the impact of Jeannie Robertson's performances derived from the depth of her imaginative and spiritual commitment to transferring the themes and motifs of her material, within their original cultural context, to a new audience. Exactly the same process is at work in Duncan Williamson's storytelling. The nature of his performance is accurately described by the storyteller and scholar Barbara McDermitt:

Each tale is told dramatically and vividly with an intenseness
and directness that draws you in and holds you riveted until

the tale's end. Duncan's verbal facility is edged with a razor sharp timing, and his large powerful hands punctuate his stories with strength and subtlety. He knows how to build suspense, bring out humour and release emotions both tragic and joyful. One cannot listen placidly to Duncan's stories. This is also true of his ballads and songs. He treats them as dramatic stories set to music and sings them with true feeling. Whether Duncan is telling a tale or sharing a ballad, he does so with such personal impact, you feel he is offering part of himself, an unforgettable gift and, as listener, you cannot help but be touched deeply by the experience.[52]

Again there is a bridging of psychological and social divisions to energise a sense of shared humanity.

But who were the audiences clustering around these master artists of a tradition that had supposedly died out a century before? The activities of Calum Maclean, Hamish Henderson and their colleagues brought scholarly attention to bear on surviving oral tradition bearers, not just in Gaelic speaking areas and among the Scottish Travellers, but in the North-east Lowlands, the Borders and the Shetlands. These were primarily rural or island traditions and the artists recorded included agricultural labourers, fishermen, shepherds, crofters and farmers – men and women. But the activity of scholarly folklorists took place against the background of the Scottish literary Renaissance and, in the sixties and seventies, of a folk revival. These related trends provided live and broadcast contexts in which traditional artists could reach outside their communities of origin to actively interested audiences. What these audiences received was not just the materials of a long-lasting culture – songs, music and story – but the mode of that culture, that is, oral transmission.

The folk revival, however, contained many other strands such as urban folk traditions based on chapbooks, broadsheets and broadside ballads; the culture of working class organisations, including the trade unions, the cooperative movement and the Workers' Educational Association; and an impulse towards radical popular protest that reached from the eighteenth- and nineteenth-century weavers to the Campaign for Nuclear Disarmament and sixties protestors against the Polaris missile.[53] Into this crucible the traditional artists poured their sources and methods, as well as a strong sense of community values. This constituted a kind of radical conservatism or conservative radicalism which affirmed communal solidarity, equality, justice and freedom. Within the folk revival pivotal figures, such as Hamish Henderson and Ewan McColl, linked the rural artists with contemporary radical songsters, such as Matt McGinn, Morris Blythman and Adam MacNaughton. This was possible because Henderson and McColl were themselves scholar-collectors, song-makers and political activists combined.

Storytelling in its own right was not prominent in the folk revival of the seventies in comparison with song and instrumental music. It was not until the work of the Traveller storytellers began to be published that they were invited to schools and other venues to share their traditions. In the late eighties, the Netherbow Arts Centre in Edinburgh began to feature traditional storytelling and a Scottish Storytelling Festival was founded. Oral storytelling began to move beyond the previous limits of the Folk Revival and to engage with a wider community of contemporary audiences. At the same time, traditional music began to invade listeners beyond the confines of the folk enthusiasts.

With the birth of the Scottish Storytelling Festival in 1989, audiences began to experience a range of oral narrative, including traditional storytellers from different parts of Scotland, storytellers from other cultures and some storytellers who developed their material from contemporary experience. What remained constant was a deep respect for the traditional cultural sources and a commitment to oral crafting, improvisation and delivery, as the defining method or art form. But it quickly became apparent that a Storytelling Festival was not enough. Of necessity, storytelling broke down the artificial barrier between performer and audience to create an environment of interaction and participation. Out of this new energy in 1990, came the

Guid Crack Club, a monthly storytelling gathering open to all-comers, and in 1992, a Scottish Storytelling Forum, embracing established storytellers, enthusiasts and learners, teachers, librarians, ministers, social workers and country-side rangers. The 'rediscovered' live art of storytelling was taken into schools, libraries, care centres, forests, camp sites, museums and art centres. Funding bodies began to take notice and more people began to think of themselves as storytellers.[54] In 1997, the George Mackay Brown Scottish Storytelling Centre was set up by the Storytelling Forum at The Netherbow to resource and develop this expanding network.

It is arguable that these developments involved a diminu-tion or dilution of tradition. Certainly individuals came to claim the storytelling mantle without understanding the inherent dynamics and discipline of the art form. Tradi-tional materials were sometimes applied without respect to their character or the integrity of their social contexts. Nonetheless, these risks were balanced by the energy of new inclusion and by the integrity of a process which enabled new kinds of interaction, as well as the development of the art form in fresh contexts. Perhaps this kind of process was always a necessary part of any living cultural tradition.

The rediscovery and then, to some extent, revival of oral storytelling was, therefore, a cumulative process with succes-sive stages. But did it have any significance for the overall reshaping of Scotland's story? Clearly issues of identity within an increasingly globalised culture were a significant factor. The telling, receiving and shaping of stories contributes towards people finding their place in the world; through narrative the variety of human experience can be explored and people come to see the world in different ways. By storytelling, people become engaged in finding their own story and voice but also in seeing how this is related to the sum of human lives. Political, social, economic and cultural change in twentieth-century Scotland stimulated this kind of questioning, though the identities explored might be local, regional, national, international or all of these in combina-tion.

Another dimension of the storytelling experience is much more rooted in place and environment. Traditional story-telling is a form of cultural ecology in which human memory encodes and passes on landscape forms, flora, fauna and the nature–culture interface through visual imagery, language and narrative structures. The natural environment influences the culture-shaping story while myths and legends, in turn, affect how people read and relate to the landscape. In her ground-breaking study of Renaissance culture, *The Art of Memory* (1992),[55] Frances Yates argues that vital and living images reflect the vitality and life of the environment, unify the contents of memory and set up 'magical' correspondences between outer and inner worlds. This is clearly demonstrated in the contemporary work of the Skye story-teller, George MacPherson, who has played a significant part in Scottish recovery of traditional storytelling. MacPherson's repertoire embodies the history and ecology of his Glendale home, animating the social, psychological and natural worlds as a single living whole.[56]

On this model, biodiversity and cultural ecology hang together and Scottish storytelling, in all its facets, may be integral to how we see our environment in relation to human identity. Interdependence and sustainability are the keynotes in a cultural continuum that is important to health and survival. Scottish Travellers and Hebridean tradition bearers alike are threatened or marginalised cultural species because Scotland's industrial and, to some extent, post-industrial values are unsustainable. People were drawn to the Traveller storytellers because they sensed that their narratives embodied genuine alternatives – fragile survivals that may carry a significance in inverse proportion to their lack of cultural status or pretension. In two finely illustrated volumes, *The Summer Walkers* (1996) and *The Voice of the Bard* (1999), Timothy Neat advances this case for both the Traveller tradition bearers and the local bards of Gaelic culture. In the latter study Neat links such tradition bearers with the inspiration of romantic artists like Blake and Words-worth and the essays of John Ruskin. Neat's co-author and collaborator, John MacInnes, reaches back into Gaelic history to demonstrate the centrality of the tradition bearers and their remarkable continuity.[57]

Perhaps though it could be put more simply and directly. To respect the ancestors is to place the community above self; to see human life in its natural interdependence is to value all life as the necessary ground of moral and spiritual being. Respect and reverence infuse the aesthetic achievements of the tradition bearers. Far from being a simplistic assertion of racial or political identity, the storytelling art is profoundly questioning and subversive of many social presumptions. Within the panoply of late twentieth-century voices, the tradition bearers and storytellers reached into the past to affirm new possibilities for the future of Scotland.

Notes

1. See Wood, Stephen (1987), *The Scottish Soldier*, Manchester: Archive Publications, pp. 45–78.
2. See, for example, MacDuff, John R., *David Livingstone*, extracted in Bateman, Meg, Crawford, Robert and McGonigal, James (eds) (2000), *Scottish Religious Poetry: An Anthology*, Edinburgh: Saint Andrew Press, pp. 186–7.
3. See Brown, Callum R, (1997), *Religion and Society in Scotland Since 1707*, Edinburgh: Edinburgh University Press.
4. See Smith, Donald C. (1987), *Passive Obedience and Prophetic Protest*, New York: Peter Long; and Brown, S. J. (1982), *Thomas Chalmers and the Godly Commonwealth*, Oxford: Oxford University Press.
5. Muir, Edwin (1963), *Collected Poems*, London: Faber & Faber, p. 97.
6. For an attempt at non-controversial balance in this much discussed topic see Smith, Donald 'Culture and Religion' in Scott, Paul H. (ed.) (1993), *Scotland: A Concise Cultural History*, Edinburgh: Mainstream Publishing, pp. 47–60.
7. MacLean, Sorley (1972), *Spring Tide and Neap Tide: Selected Poems 1932–72*, Edinburgh: Canongate.
8. See Craig, Cairns (1999), *The Modern Scottish Novel: Narrative and the National Imagination*, Edinburgh: Edinburgh University Press.
9. See Howard, Philip (ed.) (1998), *Scotland Plays*, London: Nick Hern Books, p. ix.
10. See Hardy, Forsyth (2000), *Scotland in Film*, Edinburgh: Edin-

burgh University Press; and Petrie, Duncan (2000), *Screening Scotland*, London: British Film Institute.

11. See Dick, Eddie, Noble, Andrew and Petrie, Duncan (eds) (1993), *Bill Douglas: A Lanternist's Account*, London: British Film Institute.

12. For an accurate account of this phenomenon see Elspeth King's excellent introduction to Hamilton of Gilbertfield, William (1998), *Blind Harry's Wallace*, Edinburgh: Luath Press.

13. See D'Arcy, Julian (1999), *Scottish Skalds and Sagamen*, East Lothian: Tuckwell Press.

14. See McGrath, John (1981), *A Good Night Out: Popular Theatre: Audience, Class and Form*, London: Eyre and Methven.

15. The Roman novels include *Augustus* (1986), *Tiberius* (1990), *Caesar* (1993), and *Anthony* (1997). The contemporary European novels include *The Death of Men* (1981) and *A Question of Loyalties* (1989).

16. See Beveridge, Craig and Turnbull, Ronald (1997), *Scotland After Enlightenment*, Edinburgh: Polygon.

17. *The Modern Scottish Novel: Narrative and the National Imagination*, p. 31.

18. Watson, Roderick 'Dialectics of Voice and Place' in Scott, Paul H. (ed.) (1993), *Scotland: A Concise Cultural History*, Edinburgh: Mainstream Publishing, p. 104.

19. See Campbell, John Lorne (2000), *A Very Civil People: Hebridean Folk History and Tradition*, Edinburgh: Birlinn Press.

20. Quoted in Seán Ó Súilleabháin 'Memoir' in Maclean, Calum (1990), *The Highlands*, Edinburgh: Mainstream Publishing p. 11. *The Highlands* was originally published in 1959 and re-issued by Club Leabhar in Inverness with Ó Súilleabháin's 'Memoir' in 1975.

21. See for example Nos. 18, 55a, 58, 62a, 66b and 92 in Bruford, A. J. and MacDonald D. A. (eds) (1994), *Scottish Traditional Tales*, Edinburgh: Polygon.

22. *The Highlands*, pp. 26–9.

23. See Finlay, Alec (ed.) (1996), *The Armstrong Nose: Selected Letters of Hamish Henderson* Edinburgh: Polygon.

24. See Henderson, Hamish (ed.) (1974), *Antonio Gramsci: Letters from Prison* translated by Hamish Henderson, Edinburgh: EUSPB.

25. See Porter, James and Gower, Hershcel (1999), *Jeannie Robertson: Emergent Singer, Transformative Voice*, East Lothian: Tuckwell Press.

26. Ibid. pp. 131–2.
27. Ibid. p. 159.
28. *Scottish Traditional Tales,* pp. 55–64.
29. Douglas, Sheila (ed) (1987), *The King o The Black Art,* Aberdeen: Aberdeen University Press: Aberdeen, p. 2.
30. See Stewart, Sheila (2000), *An Ancient Oral Culture,* Scone: Sheila Stewart.
31. See Neat, Timothy (1996), *The Summer Walkers,* Edinburgh: Canongate.
32. *Scottish Traditional Tales* p. 377.
33. Ibid. pp. 377–8.
34. Whyte, Betsy *The Yellow on the Broom (1979),* Edinburgh W. R. Chambers Ltd, p. 144
35. Robertson, Stanley (1988), *Exodus to Alford,* Nairn: Balnain Books, p. 16
36. Quoted in McDermitt, Barbara 'Stanley Robertson' in *Tocher* No.40 (1986), Edinburgh: School of Scottish Studies, p. 174.
37. Ibid. p. 177.
38. Ibid. p. 181.
39. See *Traditional Tales,* pp. 244–50.
40. Ibid. pp. 247–8.
41. Ibid. p. 248.
42. Ibid. pp. 249–50.
43. Duncan Williamson has told the author this story on two different occasions with considerable emphasis and he often tells his school audiences about his Granny MacDonald.
44. See Williamson, Duncan and Williamson, Linda (1987), *A Thorn in the King's Foot,* Middlesex: Penguin Books
45. Williamson, Duncan (1992) *Tales of the Seal People,* Edinburgh: Canongate, p. 99.
46. Ibid. p. 135.
47. See *A Thorn in the King's Foot;* Williamson, Duncan (1983), *Fireside Tales of the Traveller Children,* Edinburgh: Canongate; and Williamson, Duncan (2000), *The King and the Lamp,* Edinburgh: Canongate.
48. *A Thorn in the King's Foot,* pp. 270–1.
49. See Williamson, Duncan (1987), *Tell Me a Story for Christmas,* Edinburgh: Canongate, pp. 115–17.
50. See *A Thorn in the King's Foot,* pp. 113–22.
51. Ibid. pp. 258–64.
52. Quoted in Ibid. pp. 28–9.
53. See Buchan, Norman 'Folk and Protest' in Cowan, Edward J.

(ed.) (1980), *The People's Past: Scottish Folk, Scottish History*, Edinburgh: Polygon; and Henderson, Hamish (1992) *Alias MacAlias: Writings on Songs, Folk and Literature*, Edinburgh: Polygon, pp. 1–18.

54. See *Storytelling in Scotland*, (1997 and 2000) Edinburgh: Scottish Storytelling Centre. Between these two editions the number of people recognised as professional storytellers in Scotland by the Centre rose from 37 to 70.

55. See Yates, Frances A. (1992), *The Art of Memory*, London: Pimlico.

56. See MacPherson, George W. (2001), *Highland Myth and Legend*, Edinburgh: Luath.

57. See Neat, Timothy with MacInnes, John (1999), *The Voice of the Bard*, Edinburgh: Canongate, pp. 321–52.

New Enlightenment?

———◆———

When something important happens in Scotland there is an instinct to express it in buildings – making, repairing or demolishing. If someone important is to be recognised, then monuments are built in stone. Perhaps only stone can endure the northern climate and give some comfort in the face of exposure and fragility. But, in a technologically driven twenty-first century, the significance of place is under question. Has identity become a mobile quality, subject to individual choice and consumer construction? Is a virtual reality of Scotland, in, for example, the perceptions of the North American Scots diaspora, more important than topographical reality or cultural locality? Do we have a menu of narrative options from which we can select Scotland's futures or are geography and climate still determining factors?

Scotland's capital city Edinburgh clings to the eroded remnants of a single massive volcano. Millions of years of weather have left three distinct hills – Arthur's Seat, Castle-hill and Calton Hill – and a network of slopes and gullies. The slopes and gullies are peopled with stone shelters but anything of collective significance clusters around the three hills. So, if in 2000 a new era has begun in Scotland, we may see some evidence on these hills. Moreover, if we can read the stones we may garner some clues about the nature of the change and judge how it may measure up against those older Scottish tests – time, weather and wellbeing.

The largest of Edinburgh's three hills is Arthur's Seat, which has eventually shrugged off all attempts at human habitation. Hill forts, chapels and farming homesteads have crumbled into the landscape though the practised eye can trace cultivation terraces still looped around the mountain's flanks. Eventually royal power settled for a game reserve and planted a residence at Holyrood between the city and the land, evidently claiming both as personal domains. Power processed from here up the Canongate, through ceremonial entry at the Netherbow, to parliament, burgh, castle fortress and prison.

Now try the journey in reverse. Trail down the tourist mile to arrive . . . where? A beautiful period palace where no royal power resides, flanked, until recently, by a brewery headquarters and public toilets. But this legacy has been torn down. The giant claw of demolition has cleared the building site of decaying teeth and suddenly opening out at journey's end is the Palace of Holyrood House, set in a vista of hill and sky. The site has been cleared for a parliament building which will make a new claim of right in relation both to land and people. Scotland's new era is being embodied in the bold design of Catalan architect, the late Enric Miralles, with swathes and curves of stone and wood and glass, following the curves of land and sky out to sea. Like Scotland's new era this project has a dreamlike air, the atmosphere, like Referendum Day 1997, when polling stations closed to empty streets and everybody held their breath. But, day by day, the yawning gap has been filled with new construction beneath a forest of cranes. This parliament will be a monument in stone but you need to look at Edinburgh's other hills to find out why.

Two bridges throw their spans across the gullies to reach Calton Hill. North Bridge and Waterloo – the latter built by a lighthouse-building Stevenson, who grandfathered Robert Louis Stevenson – are triumphs of the engineering art. These are North British routeways, transporting Scottish industry and commerce into a later global empire. In 1815, the newly opened bridge becomes a triumphal arch for Wellington's bloody defeat of Napoleon and France's bid to lead a new European order. Nothing, it appears, can halt this onward march as the bridge soars over the old road to Leith and slices through the Calton graveyard. But Monuments in stone survive and Calton is a hill of monuments, especially this surviving graveyard hillock of the dead.

The perfect cylinder of David Hume's monument invites a moment's contemplation yet seems to reserve as much as it reveals. Harried as 'the notorious atheist', Hume took the precaution of financing his own memorial and arranging for Robert Adam to design it. Prudent Davie! In fact, such was the fuss surrounding his death in 1776, relations stood guard at night. The main offence seems to have been Hume's equable resolve in the face of untreatable stomach cancer – a circumstance morbidly related by James Boswell, who could not resist the compulsive fear of death, going with prostitutes on Calton Hill or a good hanging. The courage and significance of Hume is his commitment to a life of reason, though he understood humanity to be the slave of prejudice and passion. Hume's scepticism defies the false claims of science, religion, philosophy or politics to absolute truth and makes our fragile humanness the measure of all things. This modest voice has gone on speaking in slightly clearer tones throughout this century of devastation by competing certainties and speaking with a Scottish accent.

Ironically, Hume's restraint is overshadowed by the towering Cleopatra's needle of the Martyr's Monument. Sentenced in 1796 to fourteen years in Botany Bay, Thomas Muir and his radical compatriots – the Friends of the People – were afire with certainty about man's inherent rights and the need to reclaim the liberty that was their birthright. Hume would have smelled anarchy and invoked the rights of property, but he would not have condoned the scandal of a Scottish judge condemning political belief as a crime. 'The British Constitution,' snarled Lord Braxfield, 'is the best that ever was since the creation of the world, and it is not possible to make it better.' The line was held till Revolutionary France was beaten and reform could no longer be denied as treason.[1]

Of course Tory author, sheriff and grandee, Walter Scott, cheered Braxfield on, doing his own bit by putting down the Gala weavers. But, when Robert Burns rose to his feet in Dumfries's Theatre Royal to sing 'Ca Ira', he was investigated by his government employers and had to bite his tongue or face dismissal. Those employers – or at least their successors – now occupy the side of Calton Hill with St Andrew's House alongside the Burns Monument, which looks as if it is still biting its tongue in a Grecian kind of way. Rabbie's stone obelisk is a tribute to the muses and prettily eschews any reference to philosophy or politics. But what is 'A Man's a Man For a That' if not a circular definition of natural rights? When Burns heard of Thomas Muir's transportation, he penned 'Scots wha hae wi Wallace Bled', having been 'roused into writing it by the recollection of that glorious struggle for liberty associated with the glowing ideas of other struggles not quite so ancient'.[2]

Between St Andrew House, now being renovated to serve the new Scottish government, and the Burns Monument is Thomas Hamilton's Greek revival masterpiece, the Royal High School. First upgraded in 1979 to seat the devolution parliament that never was, this is a building spurned and in search of a role. But it occupies the hillside with calm repose and no hint of apology. Here, at the gates, the democracy vigil continued from 1992, when a diminishing Scottish Conservative Party enjoyed its fourth successive elevation to the governance of Scotland, until the referendum victory. That makes 1,979 days, reversing 1979 into 1997. Could mathematical harmony be inherent in the universe? But, as yet, there is no monument – the vigil's hut has been cleared away – and no trace remains of democracy's stubborn foot soldiers. But the Grecian theme accompanies our ascent of Calton Hill. From Hamilton's Royal High School to the uncompleted National Monument and Playfair's classical observatory as Greek Temple, culminating in the lucid perfection of the Monument to Dugald Stewart, which imitates a similar monument on the Acropolis. What is this obsession with being Greek?

The aspiration to be the 'Athens of the North' is more important in the making of modern Scotland than romantic nationalism. An Acropolis city espouses democracy, learning, philosophy and the arts, so Calton Hill is temple mount, citadel, theatre and the site of political assembly. In the full-blown myth, a northern Athens evinces hardihood in the Spartan mode, while our brains are stimulated by the austere air and our sight sharpened by clear light! Even our language is the Doric, plain, strong, honest, albeit home-spun speech. This is laughable but classical idealism is all pervasive in Scottish culture from the medievals to the moderns, shaping a distinctive north European humanism, while our built heritage reaffirms the message at every turn.

But things get more complicated still. Doric is also the North British mode, since the Athens of the North is a distinctive part of the political Union project with England, though not yet with Europe. This cause is promoted in the English language by poets, novelists, historians, natural and social scientists and philosophers who, together, can make Scotland the best regarded place for literature in Europe. Hume's boast was that, in his day, this objective had been achieved.[3] The parallel danger however was that, with a failure of political or cultural will, the North British project could lapse into anglicisation for its own sake and compla-cent mediocrity. The National Monument which aimed to be Scotland's Parthenon remains fragmentary and incom-plete and was labelled in its own time 'Edinburgh's dis-grace'. Was there, then, a failure of nerve?

Edinburgh's disgrace highlights another problem which the eighteenth century had not foreseen. While the philo-sophers were progressive in politics and sympathetic to American independence, the nineteenth century increas-ingly drew Scotland into the imperial expansion of Britain. Trade and empire went together, fuelling rapid industrial-isation which, in turn, was the main cause of cultural change in Scotland. Already, in the eighteenth century, the political management of Scotland was financed through Indian trade and the military jobbery that came with empire. Edinburgh's Parthenon was constructed as a memorial to the dead of the Napoleonic Wars. Since these wars aimed not just at re-straining French ambitions but at the final suppression of the French Revolution abroad and the radical cause at home, the incompleteness of the National Monument may indicate a moment when classical ideals and politico-economic realities parted company, leaving the Scottish Parthenon stranded on Calton Hill, half-built.

This reading of the stones gains credence when you see the Napoleonic building on Calton Hill which was completed, Nelson's Monument. This remarkable viewing tower consciously imitates an upturned telescope, recalling the Battle of Copenhagen when Nelson responded to a signal to retreat by raising a telescope to his blind eye. The Monument was initiated in an outpouring of grief for the slain hero of Trafalgar at the height of British fears about a French invasion. The Admiral's telescope looks distinctly odd beside the Parthenon but, nonetheless, each building comments on the other. At the same time, Scott's poetry was reinventing even the Gaelic speaking Highlands as an adjunct of the British war effort, on the grounds that regiments recruited in this wild warrior region were leading the patriotic charge. The ground was shifting to Scottishness as a subsidiary kind of Britishness, at its worst or, at best, a form of dressing-up which Scots themselves soon learned to manipulate to advantage.

Nelson's Monument, however, has another obvious aspect which is integral to its site and profoundly relevant to the Enlightenment endeavour. The tower replaced a navigation mast and later a time ball was added which dropped at 12 noon GMT, enabling sailors to set their chronometers. Exactly the same need for more accurate navigation drove the creation of both the Old and Royal Observatories on Calton Hill. The maritime landmark could also be a viewing point for the heavens and advance practical agendas of trade and exploration as well as experimental science.

The Royal Observatory sustains the Acropolis theme since its design is based on the Theseion in Athens. In addition, in the south-east corner of the courtyard wall, the architect, William Playfair, inserted a severely Doric monument to his uncle the mathematician, John Playfair, who had initiated the project. Under Thomas Henderson (and then Charles Piazzi Smyth), the Royal Edinburgh Observatory blazed a trail for observational astronomy of the highest order. Smyth was among the first to realise the effect of atmospheric quality on his data, perhaps because Calton Hill was surrounded by Edinburgh's chimney pots. He spent his honeymoon eleven thousand feet up in Tenerife demonstrating his thesis, beginning the trend towards mountain observatories which still characterises world astronomy. Later, James Clerk Maxwell's discovery of radio waves transformed the reach of earthbound telescopes, but his scientific genius was to combine experimental method with the bold application of mathematics, so unifying two important strands of his Scottish Enlightenment inheritance.[4]

The monument to Dugald Stewart which commands the western approach to Calton Hill is an important link between the first generation of enlightenment gurus, such as Hume, Adam Smith and Thomas Reid, and the nineteenth-century scientists, social scientists, anthropologists and philosophers such as Clerk Maxwell, Kelvin, William Hamilton and William Robertson Smith. Stewart's long career as a distinguished moral philosopher and inspirational teacher ensured that succeeding generations of students were imbued with the broad mental disciplines and social awareness of what the twentieth-century philosopher, George Davie, defined as 'the democratic intellect'.[5]

Just before the descent from Calton Hill re-emerges on to Waterloo Place, a shady gateway on the right announces itself as Rock House. Here, in the 1840s, David Octavius Hill and Robert Adamson raised the newborn technology of the calotype to an artform. Calton Hill also housed the city's first public *camera obscura*, but it was the little walled garden of Rock House that provided a private studio for a uniquely Scottish fusion of science and art.[6] Hill was a key figure in Edinburgh's cultural life. Secretary of the Royal Scottish Academy, he was also a distinguished landscape painter and an illustrator of Burns's poetry. Robert Adamson came from a family of doctors and scientists but had been forced to give up engineering due to weak health. The origins of their collaboration were democratic and religious.

In 1843, more than a third of the ministers and congregations of the established Church of Scotland left rather than submit to rule by landed patrons and the Westminster House of Lords. Walking out of the Church's General Assembly in solemn procession, the rebel ministers gathered to sign a Deed of Demission – the constitutional claim of right for a new Free Church of Scotland. Hill was caught up in the excitement of this national cause and immediately began to sketch the scene for a major composition; no longer need Scottish painting look back in time for its moments of historic drama. But how could one capture the presence of so many individuals each of whom had played their dramatic part? David Brewster, inventor of the kaleidoscope, suggested using calotypes to record a portrait of each participant from which the features could be painted in later. He also suggested Adamson for technical backup.

At Rock House the task began but quickly the potential of calotype art outgrew the initial project. From Calton Hill the collaborators could see a natural, social and historic panorama of the city. To the south was the decaying, poverty-infested Old Town; to the west and east the ordered terraces of the prosperous New Town. The aim of Thomas Chalmers, leader of this ecclesiastical Disruption, was to bridge the social and economic gap by restoring parishes, even in cities, as self-reliant communities thriving on hard work and charity. To the north, on the Firth at Newhaven, was just such a community, governed by the democratic Society of Free Fishers. Hill and Adamson photographed the people of Newhaven intensively, creating a synthesis of landscape, character portrait and communal values which stands alongside Burns or Scott as a vision of one-nation Scottishness pitched against corrosive forces of economic change.[7]

Hill and Adamson's work takes visual memorialising beyond the stones, but the photography betrays a self-conscious transience. Gravestones figure frequently and Hill, who had already lost his wife, experienced both Adamson's early death and a haunting fear that the calotypes would literally fade into oblivion. The Disruption painting was not finished until 1871, long after Adamson's death, but it somehow fails to catch the excitement of Hill's first sketches. Strangely, Adamson appears in the picture as a youth and Hill as a self-portrait in old age.

Walter Scott, by contrast, is memorialised in the grandest

Victorian style stone could command. The Scott Monument stands in Princes Street Gardens midway between Calton Hill and Castlehill, pointing to the sky like a gigantic cake decoration. It is a fitting tribute to the dream factory which Scott produced with astonishing industriousness to mesmerise Britain and Europe. It is also a romance in stone to match Abbotsford, the Borders mansion into which Tory grandee Scott poured his passion, enthusiasm and money. Did Abbotsford mean more to Scott than his literary genius? Probably. Yet Scott's work, ramshackle and unwieldy though it can be, is illuminated by shafts of human sympathy and sustained by acute social and historical intelligence. Scott's novels exhibit all the contradictions of North Britishness under pressure, but also provide a vital bridge at a time when past and present, Highland and Lowland, seemed irretrievably broken apart. A phalanx of modern Scottish historians have provided new and better foundations for understanding Scotland's past, but trying to ignore Scott's theatrical and dramatic myth making is an ineffective antidote since his cultural legacy is embedded all around us, like the gardens surrounding his monument.

The ascent to Castlehill is built on a gigantic mound of earth and rock piled up to bridge the gully between the Old and New Towns. The view from the foot is remarkable. Foregrounded are the classical façade of Octavius Hill's Royal Scottish Academy, topped by a squat statue of Queen Victoria as Britannia, and Playfair's purely Grecian National Gallery. Above these temples of culture rise the towers of New College and the Assembly Hall. This is Playfair again but now in Gothic mode, providing the new Free Church with its democratic centrepiece. Between the Assembly Hall towers, the spire which Pugin designed for the established Church's Assembly Hall soars higher than the castle. Free Kirk and Auld Kirk united in Playfair's Hall in 1929, while Pugin's spire now adorns The Hub, a superbly renovated centre for the Edinburgh International Festival.

At the time of writing, the Scottish Parliament works in the General Assembly Hall, where previous generations of ministers and elders debated the state of the nation, and the

newly elected MSPs posed en masse for the cameras, recalling Octavius Hill's Disruption painting. The echoes are not
accidental since the nineteenth-century struggle for democracy and reform has more to do with the new parliament
than the network of lords, lairds and lawyers who managed
Scottish affairs in Old Parliament Hall until 1707 and contrived to continue managing them, even when their severely
limited form of representation was moved to Westminster by
the Treaty of Union. MSPs might, however, note that Thomas Chalmer's Free Church vision did not lead to a unified
nation of renewed communities but to denominational
institution building and social conflict. Chalmers devoted
his later years to working with the poorest of the poor in
Edinburgh's West Port, as if he sensed already that the result
could not meet the expectations of the dream which had led
him, like John Knox, to break the Church in pursuit of a
greater national good.[8]

The short route up Castlehill passes beneath the Outlook
Tower of Patrick Geddes. Biologist, sociologist, urban plan-
ner, educator and cultural visionary, Geddes carried Scotland's Enlightenment project into a twentieth century
dominated by the idea of evolution, as science and storytelling converged. Originally a *camera obscura* (moved from
Calton Hill), the Outlook Tower begins properly at the top
with a conspective vista of geology, landscape, human settlement, history and culture – or as Geddes liked to put it:
place, work and folk.[9] Standing on the parapet you look
south to Arthur's Seat and west to the castle rock while,
below, a hedge of spires and towers leads the eye out past the
Scott Monument and Calton Hill to the Firth of Forth and
the sea, or past St Giles and Old Parliament Hall to Holyrood.

For Geddes, this outer view was complemented by the
imagery of the *camera obscura* and by the inner eye of
meditation and reflection. Virtual reality had its place, albeit
without the immediate communicability offered by computer technology, but it had to be balanced by the biological
social and cultural ecospheres. Descending the tower you
pass through visual explorations of Edinburgh's place in

Scotland, Scotland's place in the world and, finally, of human development on a global scale. These succeeding levels were an exposition of the need to apply science, art, social science and spirituality to human understanding and decision-making, and an immediate demonstration of the method open to any citizen or student. For Geddes, the organic vitality of natural development should also energise human affairs. Geddes's Outlook Tower has been absorbed into a tourist attraction, but his thinking anticipates the complex global challenges which face Scottishness in our time and which require holistic and synergic responses. Geddes's emphasis on living organisms moves in parallel with the ecologist-naturalists such as John Muir, Frank Fraser Darling and Morton Boyd. But, in a wider frame, he brings together reason, imagination and spirit – Enlightenment, Romanticism and religion – in a way that encapsulates much of what is distinctively Scottish and belongs to the twenty-first century. Moreover, he sought to apply his thinking through community housing schemes, environmental regeneration and education in Scotland, India, Israel, Europe and America. Geddes would have relished the visual, social and cultural prospect of the Holyrood Parliament; we need to look again at the view from the Outlook Tower internally and externally.

Weaving through the tourists, you ascend the summit of the castle rock. Fortress, military headquarters and prison by turns, Edinburgh Castle is an odd symbol of romantic nationhood. The presence here of 'The Honours of Scotland' – the crown, the sword and the sceptre – does, though, seem appropriate, for the castle was a mainstay of often oppressive royal government. Today these 'Honours' are essentially baubles – a heritage showpiece and political plaything, first rediscovered and deployed by Walter Scott for the royal visit of 1822. Royal government has meant little in Scotland for two centuries and the cardboard cutout version of Scottish history kindly provided in the 'Honours' Exhibition by Historic Scotland seems to confirm a sense of unreality. Nonetheless, the sight of Scotland's premier aristocrat, the Duke of Hamilton, carrying James V's Crown to the opening of the new Scottish Parliament in 1999 was a tenacious link with the old Kingdom of Scotland. The Honours of Scotland have at least more claim to be symbols of historic continuity than their accompanying exhibit, the supposed Stone of Destiny, on which medieval Scottish kings sat to be crowned. As Edward I, Hammer of the Scots, advanced, intent on destroying this troublesome nation, the monks of Scone, guardians of the Stone and its coronation rites, were not idle. The real Stone is probably buried somewhere on a Perthshire hillside, while the shapeless and unadorned lump of local sandstone on display in Edinburgh Castle was handed over in its place.

The concept of political sovereignty may become as insignificant in an interdependent world as the physical Stone of Destiny. More importantly, medieval Scotland gave the modern nation the powerful idea of the community of the realm preserving the common wealth or common guid. This community had frequently to be asserted against the exercise of arbitrary royal power. We hear it in the voice of Sir David Lyndsay's John the Commonweal condemning the 'Thrie Estaitis' of government, in the presbyterian sonorities of the National Covenant and in the Claim of Right of 1988 which paved the way for the Scottish Constitutional Convention and devolution. The Scottish Parliament must articulate and defend the community of the realm, but parliament is one part of the modern civil society in which this community is vested and not its sole embodiment. Hopefully, MSPs are well briefed on their political and constitutional roots.

In what then seemed the dark days of the eighties after the failed Referendum of 1979, the educational reformer R. F. Mackenzie took up his pen to ruminate on the nature of Scottishness. By this time Mackenzie, who was controversially suspended from his post as head teacher of Summerhill Academy in Aberdeen in 1974, had seen his philosophy of education spurned in the state system and his own views and career marginalised within a hostile political climate.[10] But his last book *A Search for Scotland* (1989), is not the work of a bitter or disillusioned man. Travelling across Scotland,

Mackenzie dug deeply into what makes Scotland Scottish and celebrated the enduring possibilities of a culture which had both nurtured and to some extent defeated him.

The core of *A Search for Scotland* is the chapter on Fife, which draws on R. F. Mackenzie's defining experience as head teacher of Braehead Junior Secondary School in Buckhaven – the 'State School' of his best known educational work.[11] Throughout *A Search for Scotland*, Mackenzie displays a fine descriptive gift in response to landscape and atmosphere:

> On a March evening, under the power of a snell north-east wind, the dark wall of an oncoming wave, darker even than the aquamarine of the sky overhead, breaks into a white line racing along the top of the wave and briefly a curtain of spray is blown off this white top into a continuous band above the wave . . . The equinoctial tide is far out on Shell Bay and we walked a long way over the pools, shifting stones and watching communities of buckies and small crabs scurrying away as the coal-black water cleared. There were hermit crabs, red weed, a shag, a dead eider duck, empty tins, a tomato sauce bottle and, washed well up the beach, an oil drum, still watertight, seaweed torn from its moorings, pieces of wood and a primus stove. Inland, an owl flew so softly and effortlessly that the silence arrested attention; it is as if somebody beside you is speaking but not a word comes out of his mouth. The owl did a skillfully executed banking turn and sat motionless on a post as it if were part of it.[12]

These passages have led to some confusion about Mackenzie's book: my own second-hand copy was classified by the Benedictine monks of Fort Augustus Abbey under 'topography'. But, in Scottish terms at least, landscape and environment are rarely neutral quantities. Like the traditional storytellers, Mackenzie is most concerned with the human factor:

> I was a schoolteacher in Fife for sixteen years and tried to communicate to the pupils (sons and daughters of miners,

factory workers, forge workers, linoleum workers, motor mechanics, shopkeepers) an awareness of this parcel of earth on which they had found themselves. In the summer term the school chaplain, the Rev. Robin Mitchell who was the BBC's bird-man, took the pupils on country walks through Keil's Den and over to Pitscottie. For the first ten minutes they listened to him as he drew their attention to wood anemones and the pink-tinted samaras of the elm and the song of the robin redbreast (a 'wee trickle of notes') and then they assumed independence and began to ferret things out for themselves. They once discovered a dozen pheasant's eggs cooked in the ashes of a tinker's fire that the tinker had covered over and forgotten or disowned. They were enjoying the freedom of the countryside. 'Freedom is a noble thing', said Barbour, the father of Scottish poetry. 'Freedom makes man to have liking.' The pupils, freed from classroom pressures, became different people, relaxed, smiling, reacting more sensuously to the natural world. Sometimes in their exuberance they hardly noticed Mitchell but it was he who had noiselessly pulled back this gauzy curtain and let them into a new world. He was unobtrusive, an enabler.[13]

To experience at first hand is, for Mackenzie, the basis of all education, but this involved not just the close-up of 'a dozen pheasant's eggs cooked in the ashes of a tinker's fire' but the bigger visual picture. A group of Braehead pupils are taken on an aerial reconnaissance of Fife, but the picture which emerges, though impressive, is still frustratingly two-dimensional, since time is missing:

It was not so easy for the pupils to visualise their position in time. I scrabbled through the history books trying to assemble a serial story that would put them in the picture. There were Fife's raised beaches at the twenty-five, fifty and hundred feet marks where people had lived when the glaciers had retreated in 8000 BC. I watched an archeologist as he delicately stroked away with a paintbrush the sand from the skull of an Iron Age figure unearthed from the sands of Largo Bay, and I tried to visualise these sea-sand burials and a stooping mourner from whose cloak a metal cloak-pin was the only other material evidence of the nature of their lives. And to recreate the circumstances of the emergency in which Vikings stashed away treasure of silver, scale armour, shield, sword-hilt and part of a sword. In 1817 a tinker found them on Norrie's Law and sold some of the silver to a Cupar watchmaker. Pitscottie's diaries tell about James III's and James IV's Scotland and the battle in the Forth, 'terrible to see'. All the woods of Fife were felled to build the three-feet thick walls of James IV's ship, the *Great Michael*.[14]

Mackenzie would have recognised, immediately, the potential of computer technology to help visualise and collate this data.

Yet this picture, now filled out three dimensionally, is still not enough. What are the processes that drive and effect change? This is the why question which resounds through Scotland's centuries from the aetiological myths and legends of tradition bearers, to medieval philosophers, to Calvinist catechists, Enlightenment philosophers and scientists, to Keir Hardie and the founding fathers of Socialism, and twentieth-century head teachers. Why and also how? For Mackenzie's pupils, history was seen as 'the transaction of remote characters in parliament and council chambers, an unintelligible performance in which they and their parents have no say'. Science and environmental studies were a matter of abstraction – 'Kirkcaldy's water supply' – unilluminated by reference to the concrete and the physical. Yet the raw material of understanding was to hand.

Farther west on Largo Bay, Buckhaven too had been a fishing village but those days were over. It wasn't often that the pupils were able to follow in clear detail the steps by which the present has emerged from the past, how a human community adapts to a changed environment in order to survive, switching over to a different way of life, the biology of the metamorphosis of a fishing village into a coal town. It was like studying the succession of movements by which a lobster jettisons its old shell and grows another. The Town Clerk of

Buckhaven and Methil lent the school a model of the new sea-town that was to take the place of the derelict fishing village. Only a generation earlier, the foreshore was covered with golden sands and the houses, picturesque as a Cornish village, enclosed it and clambered up the slope beyond. Between the school and the edge of the slope down to the sea there was a grassy patch called 'the verandah' from which our forebears looked out beyond the red tiles and white and red and black walls of the fishermen's houses to the sweep of the Fife coast from Leven to Macduff's Castle to the Wemyss Caves and the sparkle of the sea and, on a clear day, to the Lothian coast twelve miles away. But there came a day in the Industrial Revolution when the local council let the mine-owners sink a coal shaft close to the sea. As the pit bing of refuse grew, the tides of the Forth swept it out into the estuary and back towards the shore, distributing the black silt over the golden sands, filling up an open-air swimming pool and separating the lifeboat station by a pile of refuse from even the highest turmoil of the waves.[15]

Mackenzie then describes a teaching session in which pupils pored over the model and discussed the plans:

'Where would they hang their washing?' asked a practical girl, anchored in the year of the discussion, 1959. The teacher said that there would be spin-dryers. 'Will there be boats on the shore?' another pupil asked. It was a significant question. The fishermen had gone to work in the pits but many of them still had their roots in the sea. The teacher hoped there would still be boats. 'If they plant grass, how will they keep high tides from covering the grass and killing it?' The teacher said they would build a sea wall. 'But if there is a sea wall, how will you get to your boat?'[16]

The political implication of Mackenzie's approach is clear. The children are intelligent and questioning, yet they have already been marked down by the education system and are unlikely to play any part in the decision-making processes of their own society. Mackenzie goes on to quote Adam Smith, the Enlightenment philosopher and economist who was born and brought up just along the road from Buckhaven in Kirkcaldy:

> By that which a person does all day long, he is formed. His work forms him. And if you give him mindless work, he becomes a mindless person. And he cannot become a good citizen, he cannot be a good father in the family, or mother for that matter. But to become totally reduced through mindless work is the fate of the great majority of the people in all the progressive countries.[17]

At the start of the twenty-first century this could be amended to read 'mindless work or mindless leisure'. Against this Mackenzie advocates 'weighing consumer satisfactions against a simpler lifestyle and contemplating new frameworks of society'. Scotland, he argues, could become again 'a clearing house of ideas' based on a community of citizens rather than a state of subjects. The future depends on a 'tenderness towards all natural life' and 'an understanding of the terms on which we will be permitted to bide on the earth'. The possibility of change is there for Mackenzie even though in 1987, he was pessimistic about the political prospects.

In 1997, the people of Scotland chose by democratic means to establish their own national forum of political decision making. But this was the beginning rather than the end of hard choices in the face of climatic and economic forces over which the Scottish people, far less their political representatives, have little control. Scotland's principal resources are our natural environment combined with the social and cultural possibilities implicit in our inheritance. Invention without tradition is a technical gesture; tradition without innovation stultifies human capacity.

A Search for Scotland is the fruit of a lifetime's exploration, reflection and practical experience. It is a key twentieth-century text and all the more interesting because it was written before the swift political changes of 1997–9 enabled a new start for Scottish democracy. In his search, Mackenzie brings together the spirituality of the tradition bearers, Enlightenment reason and questioning, the narrative imagination of the history makers, and a characteristic Scottish determination to root knowledge and imagination in the life of society. Mackenzie's achievement is a reconciliation of narratives and a challenge to the idea that any individual story or scenario will do in a world of multiple possibilities. Wellbeing is inescapably biological, social and cultural; technology changes how we perceive and communicate these factors but cannot replace them. In the best case scenario, technology can increase democratic understanding and participation in shaping the future.

Storytelling and story making will be integral to this process because stories engage memory and imagination in the common purposes of life. Stories move complex factors together in time and contain conflicting interests within a shared narrative in search of resolution. Within that framework, oral tradition offers a remarkable thread of continuity, a celebration of landscape and a persistent reaffirmation that giving life to the future is what animates our human existence. Present day Scots have a rare opportunity to imagine the future in an interval of hope.

Notes

1. See Bewley, Christina (1981), *Muir of Huntershill* Oxford: Oxford University Press; and Mathieson, W. L. (1910), *The Awakening of Scotland,* Glasgow: James Maclehose.
2. See Crawford, Thomas (1990), *Boswell, Burns and the French Revolution,* Edinburgh: Saltire Society.
3. See Mossner, Ernest Campbell (1980), *The Life of David Hume,* 2nd edition, Oxford: Clarendon Press, pp. 356–89.
4. See Goldman, Martin (1983), *The Demon in the Aether: The Story of James Clerk Maxwell,* Edinburgh: Paul Harris.
5. See Davie, George (1961), *The Democratic Intellect: Scotland and her Universities in the Nineteenth Century* Edinburgh: Edinburgh University Press.
6. See Stevenson, Sarah (1981), *David Octavius Hill and Robert Adamson* Edinburgh: National Galleries of Scotland.
7. See Stevenson, Sarah (1991), *Hill and Adamson's The Fishermen*

and Women of the Firth of Forth, Edinburgh: Scottish National Portrait Gallery.

8. See Brown, S. J. (1982), *Thomas Chalmers and the Godly Commonwealth*, Oxford: Oxford University Press.

9. See 'Patrick Geddes: Ecologist, Educator, Visual Thinker' in Macdonald, Murdo (ed.) (Summer 1992), *The Edinburgh Review* Issue 88; and Boardman, Philip (1978), *The Worlds of Patrick Geddes*, London: Routledge and Kegan Paul.

10. See Murphy, Peter P. A. (1998), *The Life of R. F. Mackenzie*, Edinburgh: John Donald; and Mackenzie, R. F. (1976), *The Unbowed Head*. Edinburgh: EUSPB.

11. See Mackenzie, R. F. (1970), *State School*, London: Penguin Books.

12. Mackenzie, R. F., *A Search for Scotland*, Edinburgh: Collins, p. 148

13. Ibid. pp. 149–50.

14. Ibid. pp. 151–2.

15. Ibid. pp. 155–6.

16. Ibid. p. 157.

17. Quoted in Ibid. p. 165.

Index
